STUFF! GOOD SYNTH PLAYERS SHOULD KNOW

SHOULD KNOW

Take your playing from ordinary to EXTRAORDINARY!

by Mark Harrison

AN A to Z GUIDE TO GETTING BETTER

ISBN 978-1-4234-5768-8

HAL•LEONARD® CORPORATION

7777 W. BLUEMOUND RD. P.O. BOX 13819 MILWAUKEE, WI 53213

In Australia Contact:
Hal Leonard Australia Pty. Ltd.
4 Lentara Court
Cheltenham, Victoria, 3192 Australia
Email: ausadmin@halleonard.com.au

Visit Hal Leonard Online at
www.halleonard.com

CONTENTS

INTRODUCTION

Welcome to STUFF! GOOD SYNTH PLAYERS SHOULD KNOW. This book/CD package is chock-full of techniques to help your synthesizer programming and performance become more professional. We delve into both physical (stand-alone) keyboard synths and virtual software synths that run on today's fast computers. Just dive into the alphabetic list of "tips" to learn what you need to know, from Synthesis Types (analog, digital, softsynth) to Synthesis Methods (additive, subtractive, wavetable, and more) to Synthesizer Functions (attack, envelope, filter and more)… not to mention Musical Uses of Synths (arpeggiator, comping, lead, and more) and Musical Styles using Synths (house, progressive rock, techno, and more)… you get the idea! Most of the tips have accompanying CD tracks to further enhance the learning process.

Have fun playing your *Stuff* on the synthesizer!

– Mark Harrison

ABOUT THE CD

On the accompanying CD, you'll find recordings of all the music examples in the book. Most of the tracks feature a full band, with the rhythm section on the left channel and the featured synth part on the right channel. To play along with the band on these tracks, simply turn down the right channel. The CD tracks were created with the Logic, Digital Performer, and Reason workstation software programs (see individual entries for these), using a variety of hardware and software synthesizers/instruments.

ABOUT THE AUTHOR

Mark Harrison studied classical piano as a child, and by his teenage years was playing in various rock bands in his native southern England. In the 1980s he began writing music for TV and commercials, including a piece that was used for the British Labor Party ads in a national election. He also appeared on British television (BBC) and became a fixture on London's pub-rock circuit.

In 1987 he relocated to Los Angeles to experience the music business in the U.S.A. He soon began performing with top musicians such as Jay Graydon (Steely Dan), John Molo (Bruce Hornsby band), Jimmy Haslip (Yellowjackets), and numerous others. Mark currently performs with his own contemporary jazz band (the Mark Harrison Quintet) as well as with the Steely Dan tribute band Doctor Wu. His recent TV music credits include *Saturday Night Live*, *The Montel Williams Show*, *American Justice*, *Celebrity Profiles*, *America's Most Wanted*, *True Hollywood Stories*, the British documentary program *Panorama*, and many others.

Mark is also one of the top contemporary music educators in Los Angeles. He taught at the renowned Grove School of Music for six years, instructing hundreds of musicians from around the world. Mark currently runs a busy private teaching studio, catering to the needs of professional and aspiring musicians alike. His students include Grammy winners, hit songwriters, members of the Boston Pops and Los Angeles Philharmonic orchestras, and first-call touring musicians with major acts.

Mark's music instruction books are used by thousands of musicians in over 20 countries, and are recommended by the Berklee College of Music for all their new students. He also writes Master Class articles for *Keyboard* and *How to Jam* magazines, covering a variety of different keyboard styles and topics. Please visit Mark at *www.harrisonmusic.com* for information about his educational products and services, as well as his live performance activities and schedule.

ADDITIVE SYNTHESIS

Additive synthesis is the process of adding various upper partials to a fundamental frequency. Naturally occurring acoustic sounds (e.g., notes played on a piano or guitar) consist of a fundamental frequency plus a series of harmonics (or overtones, see harmonic, p. 52). Additive synthesis can re-create this process electronically to emulate existing acoustic sounds, or to create new sounds that don't have an acoustic equivalent. Perhaps the best-known "additive" instrument is the electronic organ, which uses nine different drawbars to control the mix of harmonics in the sound. (The Hammond organ was invented in the 1930s as an electronic substitute for the much larger pipe organ.)

In additive synthesis, the upper partials can be either harmonic (exact mutiples of the fundamental frequency) or inharmonic (unrelated to the fundamental frequency). Instruments such as bells and gongs have a lot of inharmonic partials, which is why these instruments have a less specific pitch compared to a piano or guitar. Additive and frequency modulation synthesis (see p. 45) are excellent for producing these inharmonic types of sounds.

Aside from organ-type instruments, probably the best-known synthesizer to use additive technology was the Synclavier, first introduced in the late 1970s by New England Digital. The Synclavier was a high-end instrument that was significantly ahead of its time, and was used by top artists such as Pink Floyd, Kraftwerk, Stevie Wonder, and Frank Zappa. More recently, additive synthesis was implemented in the Kawai K5000 range of synthesizers, introduced in the 1990s.

Into the 21st century, additive synthesis is alive and well in virtual (computer-based) instruments such as VirSyn's Cube, Camel Audio's Cameleon, and Concrete FX's Adder.

AFTERTOUCH

Aftertouch is the act of exerting pressure on a key of a synthesizer keyboard after the note is first played. This can then trigger a particular musical effect, such as changing the volume or tone color, or adding vibrato or tremolo. This is normally a programmable function, meaning that the aftertouch can be programmed to change the volume, tone color, etc. within a particular sound (or program) on a synthesizer. If you browse through the presets on your synth, you'll likely find some programs that already have the aftertouch programmed in this way.

Our first music example uses aftertouch to create vibrato (a regular variation in pitch, see p. 136) on a lead synth sound played over a funk groove. The vibrato is indicated by the wavy lines following each of the longer notes:

TRACK 1

Funk

Listen to this track on the CD and you'll hear that the lead synth sound is on the right channel, and the rest of the band is on the left channel. Fire up a lead synth (with aftertouch vibrato) on your axe and try playing along! This lead synth part was played using the ES2 "virtual" software synthesizer (see softsynth, p. 119) within Logic (a digital audio workstation that runs on Mac computers, see p. 67). The other instrument sounds in the backing band also come from Logic software synthesizers: the electric piano is played using the EVP88 "modeled" piano instrument (see physical modeling, p. 89) and the "fingerstyle" electric bass is played using the EXS24 software sampler (see p. 112).

Don't forget that aftertouch (like most of the synthesizer functions we'll be looking at in this book) can be programmed and performed using either a "real" physical keyboard synthesizer, or a virtual software synthesizer being played from a keyboard controller (see, p. 22).

Harmony/Theory Notes

The above progression is in the key of C minor, but the lead synth part uses a C Dorian mode (which is a B♭ major scale displaced to start on the note C). The C Dorian mode contains the note A, which is why we have natural signs before the As in measures 3–4 (as these contradict the A♭ in the key signature). Using Dorian modes within minor keys in this way is commonly done across a range of funk and jazz styles.

Our next track is in a blues shuffle style, and this time uses aftertouch to trigger an effect on an electric organ part. The Leslie speaker cabinet is a vital part of the sound's character for many organists, due to the rotating speaker that speeds up and slows down at the player's command. Various physical and virtual synths try to emulate the sound of an electric organ through a rotary speaker cabinet. In this example, the aftertouch is triggering the Leslie to change from the slow speed (a spacious, chorus-type sound) to the fast speed (a creamier, thicker, more active sound) and back again:

TRACK 2

Blues Shuffle

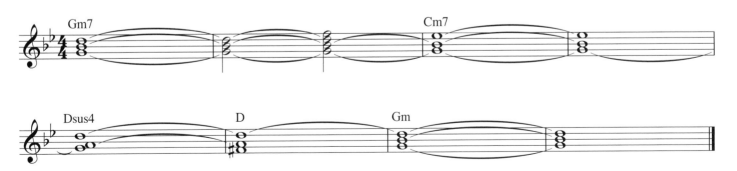

Listen to the track and you'll hear that the organ sound is on the right channel, and the rest of the band is on the left channel. You'll also notice that during measures 3–4 the rotating speaker effect starts to speed up, and during measures 7–8 the rotating speaker slows down again. This was triggered by using aftertouch on a controller keyboard. The organ part on the track is played using the EVB3 "modeled" organ instrument, another great virtual instrument within the Logic digital audio workstation software. The sound used was a "'60s Pop Organ," which has the lower drawbars pulled out (selecting the lower frequencies) and the higher drawbars pushed in (muting the higher frequencies). This results in a mellower, more rounded sound. Try playing along with this track using your favorite organ patch, and experiment with the rotary speaker effect if your instrument has that capability.

Harmony/Theory Notes

The above organ example uses an upper structure triad, which is a vital voicing technique in many contemporary styles. The right hand notes on the Cm7 chord form an E♭ major triad (E♭ G B♭). These are the 3rd, 5th, and 7th of the Cm7 chord, and can be thought of as a major triad (E♭ major in this case) built from the 3rd of the chord (Cm7 in this case). Otherwise we're using simple major and minor triads based on the chord symbols, with the 7th of the Gm7 chord being added during measure 2. The Dsus4 chord symbol signifies that the 4th (G in this case) has replaced the 3rd of the chord (F♯ in this case). This then resolves to the D major triad (containing the F♯) in the following measure.

ALESIS

Alesis is a noted manufacturer of synthesizers and electronic audio equipment. The company originated in Hollywood, California in the early 1980s. Their first hit products were the MIDIVerb (an affordable stereo reverb unit) and the MMT-8 (a multitrack MIDI recorder). These were followed by the SR-16 drum machine, which is perhaps the oldest piece of MIDI equipment still in production (although Alesis has now finally introduced an updated version, the SR-18). The SR-16 has a great selection of drum sounds and patterns, and can be found in countless home studios. I still have mine, and I use it regularly when teaching.

In 1991 Alesis introduced the ADAT multi-channel digital tape recorder, which recorded eight tracks of digital audio onto VHS video tapes. Multiple ADAT machines could also be synchronized together, enabling project studios to have 24-track capability by purchasing three ADAT machines (at a comparatively low cost). This technological and price breakthrough led to a significant growth of small and mid-size studios in the 1990s.

The ADAT tape-based recording format is now obsolete, due to the growth of computer-based recording techniques such as ProTools (see p. 100) in the 21st century. Alesis brought out a hard-disc-based successor to the original ADAT, called the ADAT HD24.

On the synthesizer front, Alesis introduced their Quadrasynth in 1993. It was a 76-key, 64-voice digital synthesizer (see p. 29) that directly connected to their ADAT recorders via an optical interface. Then in 2000 their Andromeda analog synthesizer (see p. 10) was launched. The Andromeda has analog oscillators and filters, but with modern digital controls. This instrument quickly became popular with analog synth enthusiasts for its great sound and programming capabilities.

Early in the 21st century Alesis introduced their Ion and Micron "analog modeling" synthesizers, which "model" or digitally re-create the components and sound characteristics of analog synths (see physical modeling, p. 89). Then in the mid-2000s the Fusion line of synthesizer workstations was introduced, with the combination of synthesis, sampling, and hard-disk recording (see workstation, p. 140).

AMPLIFIER

In the synthesizer world, the **amplifier** is the component that controls the volume of the sound. In basic analog synthesis (see p. 10), the amplifier stage is the last of the three main sound components, following the oscillator (see p. 86) and filter (see p. 44). The components in early synthesizers were voltage-controlled, so the amplifier stage was referred to as a voltage controlled amplifier (or VCA) in classic analog synthesizers. However, with the advent of digital synthesis (see p. 29), these synthesizer functions were re-created digitally, so the term digitally controlled amplifier (or DCA) was then used by some synth manufacturers.

The amplifier stage in a synthesizer can be controlled by two important modifiers: the envelope generator (see p. 41) and the low-frequency oscillator (LFO, see p. 71). When an envelope is applied to the amplifier stage, the volume of each note changes over time according to how the envelope is programmed. For example, a synth string sound might have a longer attack time (see p. 17) programmed in the amplifier envelope, so that the volume of the sound builds gradually once the note is played. By contrast, a punchy synth bass sound might have a short attack time programmed in the amplifier envelope, so that the full volume of the sound is heard right away.

When a low-frequency oscillator (LFO) is applied to the amplifier stage in a synthesizer, a cyclical variation in volume occurs over time (depending on the waveform and speed of the LFO, and the degree or intensity to which this is then applied to the amplifier). A typical application of this technique is to produce a tremolo effect (see p. 131).

ANALOG SYNTHESIZER

An **analog synthesizer** uses analog circuits to generate sound electronically. This is the earliest and most classic synthesizer technology, and the enduring quality and warmth of analog sounds ensure that these synths (and their digital and software-based clones) are still frequently used in the 21st century.

The earliest widely available analog synths were large modular systems that emerged in the 1960s. Their various sound components such as oscillators (see p. 86), filters (see p. 44), amplifiers (see p. 9), envelope generators (see p. 41), and low-frequency oscillators (LFOs, see p. 71) were housed in separate electronic modules, connected by patch cables. Noted modular synthesizer manufacturers included Moog (see p. 79) and ARP (see p. 12).

In the early 1970s, "all-in-one" analog synthesizers were introduced. These were integrated into a single unit, rather than using separate physical modules. The most famous and successful of these was the Minimoog (see p. 74). Back then, the processing required to generate a single note was rather complex, so most synthesizers remained monophonic (see p. 78), meaning they could play only one note at a time.

Although most of these all-in-one units did not use patch cables (as the signals were internally routed), a separate category of semi-modular synths emerged, which were all-in-one units but still offering patch cable connectivity. The most famous of these was the ARP 2600, introduced in 1971. This semi-modular architecture was also used in the Korg MS series of synths. I remember using a Korg MS-20 on various rock gigs in the United Kingdom in the late 1970s/early 1980s.

Polyphonic analog synthesizers then emerged, with the ability to play more than one note at a time (see p. 95). Notable among these early polyphonic instruments were the Oberheim Four-Voice and Polymoog synths (although the Polymoog was actually more organ-like in its design and architecture). I remember that the Polymoog was one of the hot synths to have if you were a session keyboardist in London in the late 1970s.

Around this time, another technological breakthrough came with the use of microprocessor technology in analog synstesizers. Among other things, this enabled sound programs (or "patches") to be stored in the synthesizer's memory, for instant recall during a performance. The first synths of this type were manufactured by Sequential Circuits (see p. 117), notably their groundbreaking five-voice synthesizer, the Prophet-5 (see p. 99).

By the late 1980s, analog synths had fallen out of favor, being replaced by digital synthesizers and samplers. However, in the 1990s analog sounds and synths began to have a big resurgence, fueled in part by electronic dance music and hip hop styles. Into the 21st century, analog synths are alive and well; new "hardware" analog synths are being manufactured (such as the Prophet 08 and Moog's Little Phatty), as well as virtual (computer-based) instruments emulating analog synthesis (such as Native Instruments' Pro-53, Arturia's Minimoog V, and many others).

Now we'll look at some musical examples of analog synth sounds. First up is an R&B/pop groove using a classic Minimoog-style bass sound:

R&B/Pop

Listen to the track and you'll hear that the synth bass is on the right channel, and the rest of the band is on the left channel. Try playing along with with this example, using your favorite synth bass sound. The fat and rounded sound of the Minimoog is ideal for synth bass lines in various styles. This example was produced using a Moog bass sample within the Atmosphere virtual instrument (see p. 14). This particular Moog bass uses a pulse waveform (see p. 102), which has a somewhat hollow yet warm sound characteristic. The sounds in the backing band include a staccato synth comping part and a soft analog synth pad, both from the Kontakt 3 software sampler and synthesizer (see p. 61).

Next we have a rock groove using a Roland Jupiter-style synth pad (see p. 87). The Roland Jupiter-8 (introduced in 1981) remains one of the classic analog synths of all time. (For more on this important synth, see p. 58):

TRACK 4

Rock

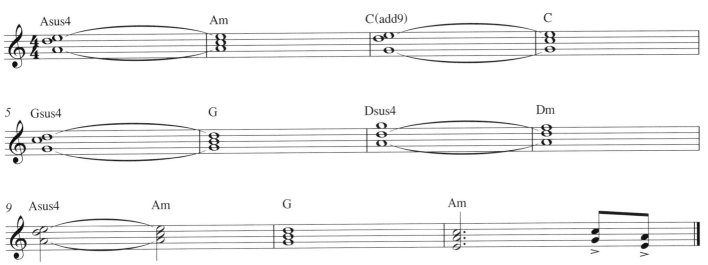

Listen to the track and you'll hear that the synth pad is on the right channel, and the rest of the band is on the left channel. This example uses a Roland Jupiter-8 synthesizer sample, again within the Atmosphere virtual instrument. In the backing band, the Kontakt 3 software sampler provides the rhythm section (bass and drums) sounds.

Harmony/Theory Notes

Notice the above synth part has some linear motion, or "interior resolutions." For example, the D in the first measure (the 4th of the Asus4 chord) resolves to the C in the second measure (the 3rd of the Am chord). Similarly, the D in the third measure (now the 9th of the Cadd9 chord) again resolves to the C in the fourth measure (the root of the C chord), and so on. This type of motion is a very effective way to spice up your synth pads and chordal parts.

ARP

ARP Instruments, Inc. was founded in 1969 by the engineer and entrepreneur Alan R. Pearlman. ARP was the main competitor to Moog Music in the synthesizer world of the 1970s. One of ARP's early landmark products was the semi-modular 2600 analog synthesizer, which could be operated either with or without patch cables (due to the internal pre-wiring of the components). The ARP 2600 was a huge success, and was used by artists as diverse as as David Bowie, Herbie Hancock, John Lennon, and Stevie Wonder. An ARP 2600 was also used to create the voice of the character R2D2 in the various *Star Wars* movies.

Hot on the heels of the 2600 came the Odyssey, introduced in 1972. This was an analog duophonic (two notes at once) synthesizer, which (unlike the 2600) was a portable performance instrument. The synth hotshots of the 1970s tended to fall into two camps: those who used the Minimoog (see p. 74) and those who used the ARP Odyssey. There was a spirited debate as to which synth sounded better, although there was some consensus that the Minimoog had a "fatter" sound due to its three oscillators, versus the Odyssey's two oscillators.

Other notable ARP synthesizers from the 1970s include:

- Omni, which had preset strings, synthesizer, and bass sounds. This was an innovative instrument for its time, and went on to become ARP's best-selling synthesizer.

- Axxe, a scaled-down version of the Odyssey, with just a single oscillator and filter.

- Quadra, which combined polyphonic synth, lead synth, bass, and string sounds.

Before the company went out of business in 1981, they developed the Chroma, a micro-processor-based analog synthesizer. Fender acquired the design of this synth, and it was eventually released as the Rhodes Chroma. This was the first commercial synthesizer with a touch-sensitive keyboard, and attracted a sizeable following in the keyboard community of the 1980s and beyond.

ARPEGGIATOR

An **arpeggiator** is a synthesizer function that generates arpeggios (broken chords) from chord voicings played on the keyboard. For example, if you play and hold a C major triad on a Korg N364 keyboard (a typical workstation synth from the mid-1990s) and hit the "Arpeggio" button, you will hear a sequence of the individual notes C, E, and G over one or more octaves, depending on the range and pattern selected. You can also control the speed of the arpeggios, and whether they play downward, upward, or in a random sequence.

The ancestor of the arpeggiator function is the hardware sequencer (see p. 116), notably the 16-step ARP Sequencer from the 1970s, which enabled an arpeggio to be repeatedly played in the studio or in live performance. Arpeggiators were implemented in many synthesizers from the late 1970s to early 1980s, including instruments such as the Roland Juno 6, Oberheim OB-Xa, and Korg Polysix. (I used a Polysix on various United Kingdom gigs and recordings in the early 1980s.)

During the heyday of digital synths in the late 1980s to early 1990s, arpeggiators largely disappeared from the scene, but they became popular again from the mid-1990s due mainly to their use in various electronic dance music styles. So from the mid-1990s into the 21st century, most synthesizers now include an arpeggiator function. What's old is new again!

Arpeggiators are also often implemented in software sequencers (see p. 116) or computer-based digital audio workstations (DAWs, see p. 26), as well as virtual instruments or soft-synths (see p. 119). Coming up we have an example of an arpeggiator being used in Reason (see p. 105), a leading digital audio workstation commonly used for electronic dance music production. Reason has an internal arpeggiator plug-in (see p. 94) called RPG-8, which was used for this example in a techno style (see p. 127). The synth voicings in measures 1–8 were also played in measures 9–16, but during these measures the RPG-8 arpeggiator was applied to this synth part, turning the voicings into a series of three-note ascending arpeggios you see in measures 9–16 of the notation:

TRACK 5

Techno

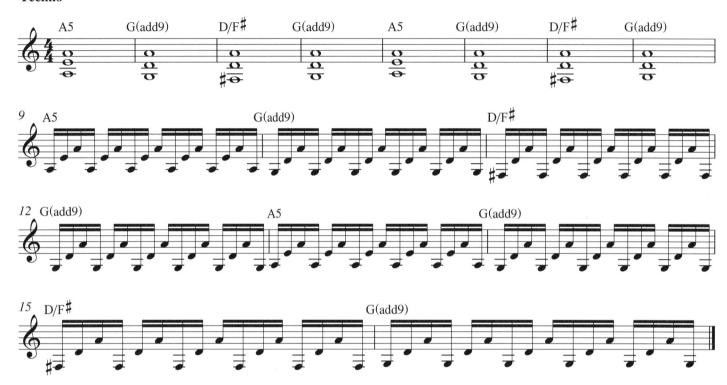

Listen to the track and you'll hear that the synth chords and arpeggios are on the right channel, and the rest of the band is on the left channel. The synth sound on the right channel is an analog/wavetable blend from the the Thor plug-in synth within Reason, called "Epic Poly." This bright synth sound is particularly suitable for electronic dance music styles. Note that the tempo of the arpeggio is synced with (matched with) the tempo of the overall sequence. This is normal for arpeggiators working inside digital audio workstation "hosts."

In the backing band, Thor is also providing the analog lead fills and techno bass sounds that you hear on the left channel. Note that the delay (echo) effect applied to the lead synth is also tempo-synched to the main sequence. This is a common and effective technique across a range of contemporary and electronic styles.

ATMOSPHERE/OMNISPHERE

Atmosphere and its successor Omnisphere are softsynths (see p. 119) or virtual instruments created by Spectrasonics, whose founder Eric Persing is one of the leading synthesists and sound designers in the world. One of the highlights of the NAMM (National Association of Music Merchants) music industry show, held in Los Angeles every year, is to see Eric holding forth about the latest Spectrasonics products to a large group of attendees and enthusiasts. Atmosphere and Omnisphere run as plug-ins (see p. 94) within a digital audio workstation host (see p. 26), such as Digital Performer, Logic, Cubase, et al.

In a crowded softsynth market, Atmosphere broke new ground in the mid-2000s as a powerful and evocative creator of lush synth textures and dynamically morphing sounds. It became a staple in studios and post-production facilities worldwide, and was used on countless movie soundtracks and trailers, TV scores, and commercial recordings. I have used Atmosphere on everything from TV documentary soundtracks to jazz-fusion CD projects, and in 2008 I "sweetened" a Christian Rock CD for a client using Atmosphere for the synth pads (see p. 87).

Omnisphere (the successor to Atmosphere) has now been released, with vastly expanded sound libraries and synthesis capabilities, and including all of the "legacy" sounds from the original Atmosphere. For me (and many other working pros), Omnisphere has become an important go-to softsynth for very usable sounds in a wide variety of styles. Stated briefly, Omnisphere rocks!

Atmosphere and Omnisphere synth sounds normally consist of two layers, each of which can be extensively edited to give an almost unlimited number of sounds. Our first music example is in an electronic/trance style, and features an Atmosphere/Omnisphere sound called "Trancey Sweep," which is created from layered samples of Roland Juno and Yamaha CS-80 synthesizers:

TRACK 6

Electronic/Trance

Listen to the track and you'll hear that the Atmosphere/Omnisphere synth pad is on the right channel, and the rest of the band is on the left channel. The sweeping effect on the synth pad is caused by an envelope (see p. 41), which causes the filter (see p. 44) to open up during the attack time (see p. 17) for each note. In the backing band, the ES2 synth plug-in within Logic (see p. 67) is providing a characteristic trance-style analog synth bass sound.

Harmony/Theory Notes

Note that the above synth part consists mainly of roots and 5ths of the various chords. (The 5 chord symbol suffix means "the root and 5th of the chord only," i.e., omitting the 3rd.) This creates a simple and transparent voicing sound, and is used in many contemporary styles—from hard-rock to electronic dance music.

Our next example is in a dramatic/film score style, and features an evolving Atmosphere/Omnisphere sound called "Vaporware Tension" that handily demonstrates this softsynth's sound morphing capabilities. This sound was created by layering samples of granular (see p. 49) and additive (see p. 6) synthesizers:

TRACK 7   **Dramatic/Film Score**

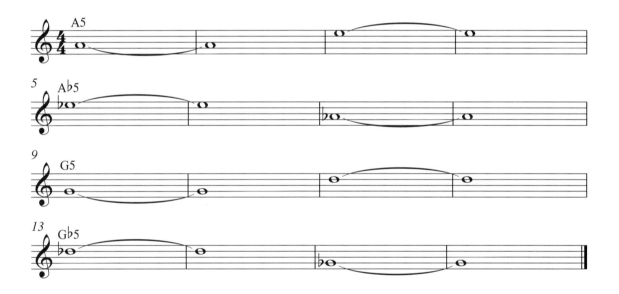

Notice how large and intricate the Atmosphere/Omnipshere synth sounds on the right channel, even though only one note is being played! The remaining instruments on the left channel consist of a bass ensemble, timpani hits and rolls, and orchestral snare drums, all from the Kontakt 3 software sampler and synthesizer (see p. 61).

ATTACK

In a synthesizer, the **attack** is the first stage of a envelope generator (see p. 41), which is a modifer normally applied to the filter (see p. 44) to control the timbre, or to the amplifier (see p. 9) to control the volume. The attack is the time taken for the envelope to reach its peak, before the decay time (see p. 25) begins.

In musical terms, a slow attack applied to a (conventional low-pass) filter means that the sound will be darker at the beginning, and then become brighter during the attack time up until the peak. By contrast, a fast attack applied to the filter means that all the harmonics/frequencies will be present right from the beginning. A slow attack applied to the amplifier means that the sound will be quieter at the beginning, and then become louder during the attack time up until the peak. By contrast, a fast attack applied to the amplifier means that the full volume of the sound will be present right from the beginning.

The recorded example on Track 8 demonstrates these principles, playing a single repeated note and using a simple sawtooth waveform (see p. 115) generated by the ES2 synth plug-in within Logic (see p. 67).

TRACK 8

The first group of four notes uses different attack times applied to the filter:

- 0 ms (milliseconds), 500 ms, 1500 ms, and 5000 ms.

The second group of four notes uses different attack times applied to the amplifier:

- 0 ms, 500 ms, 2000 ms, and 5000 ms.

In the first group of four notes, you can hear that, as the attack time increases, the sound is darker at the beginning and takes progressively longer to reach the brightness peak. In the second group of four notes, you can hear that, as the attack time increases, the sound is quieter at the beginning and takes progressively longer to reach the volume peak (without the brightness or tone color changing).

Understanding the role of the attack stage in the envelope generator is important when programming your synth. To mimic a brass sound you might typically apply a slower attack to the filter, as it takes a moment for the upper harmonics to emerge on a note played on a trumpet, for example. By contrast, to mimic a string sound you might apply a slower attack to the amplifier, as it takes a moment for the full volume to emerge on a note played on a cello.

One more thing… If you're on a recording session and the producer asks you for a shorter attack on your synth sound (with no other qualification), assume that he means the attack time within the amplifier envelope; i.e., they want the sound to "speak" right from the beginning. It's surprising how many indifferent-sounding presets on today's synths can be improved just by tweaking the attack times.

BASS LINES

One of the most important musical uses of synthesizers is to play **bass lines** in a variety of contemporary styles. You may know that synth bass is used in most forms of electronic dance music. But synth bass is also heard across a diverse range of styles such as rock, old-school R&B/funk, new age, and smooth jazz.

Our first example of a synthsizer bass line is in a funky house style (see p. 54) and uses some glide (a gradual, rather than sudden, change in pitch between successive notes; see p. 48):

TRACK 9

Funky House

Listen to the track on the CD and you'll hear that the synth bass sound is on the right channel, and the rest of the band is on the left channel. Fire up a funky synth bass sound on your axe and try playing along! This synth bass part was played using a sound called "House Stride Bass," an analog synth preset within the ES2 softsynth (a synth plug-in built into Logic). The electric piano in the backing band is played using the EVP88 "modeled" piano (see physical modeling, p. 89), another great Logic plug-in instrument.

Harmony/Theory Notes

As with all bass lines shown in this book, this example sounds an octave lower than actually written. This is for consistency with regular (i.e., non-synth) bass writing, as the bass is a transposing instrument (by one octave). Notice also that this bass line uses mostly the roots and 7ths of these minor 7th and dominant 7th chords, with some use of minor pentatonic scales. (For example, the A♭, F, and E♭ at the end of measure 1 come from the B♭ minor pentatonic scale.) This is an effective bass line technique across a range of funk/R&B and electronic dance music styles.

Our second example of a synthsizer bass line is in a synth-pop style (see p. 125) and is typical of the more keyboard-centric pop music of the 1980s:

TRACK 10

Synth-pop

Again, the synth bass sound is on the right channel, and the rest of the band is on the left channel. This is another synth bass sound from the ES2 softsynth, this time using an analog pulse waveform (see p. 102), which has a bright yet "hollow" sound characteristic.

The ES2 synth is also providing most of the backing band on the left channel, notably the staccato synth clavinet, the synth bells (measures 1–8) and the synth strings (measures 9–16). By the way, the drum loop used is in the style of the classic LinnDrum machine, a staple of many synth-pop and dance hits of the 1980s.

COMPING

Comping is a musical slang term for accompaniment. If you're not playing a bass part or lead line on your synth, you're likely to be playing some kind of comping part. Synth players will comp through a song based on their understanding of harmony and style. This involves creating stylistically appropriate voicings or figures from the chord symbols, and then playing them with a suitable rhythmic pattern. The choice of synth sound is also very important, as it needs to fit the style being played.

Our first synthesizer comping example is in a funk style, and contains two different synth parts: a staccato (short and separated) comping part in measures 1–8, and a more sustained chordal part in measures 9–16:

TRACK 11

Funk

Listen to this track on the CD and you'll hear that the synth comping parts are on the right channel, with the rest of the band on the left channel. Both of the comping synths were played using the FM8 softsynth, from Native Instruments. The FM8 uses frequency modulation or FM synthesis (see p. 45), a digital synthesis method that is great for creating bright, edgy sounds rich in harmonic content. The FM8 is the computer-based successor to the popular Yamaha DX7 synthesizer (see p. 36). The sound in measures 1–8 is "spiky" and "clavinet-like" and is suited to the sparse two-note intervals and rhythmic syncopations used in this part. By contrast, the sound in measures 9–16 is a full and bright synth pad, suitable for larger and more sustained voicings.

The rhythm section on the left channel deserves an honorable mention. The bass sound is from the wonderful Scarbee Red Bass virtual instrument, and the drums are from the BFD2 virtual drum instrument. These instruments are the state-of-the-art for bass and drums plug-ins respectively, in the late 2000s.

Harmony/Theory Notes

Note that in measures 1–8 (the synth clav part), we are playing mostly the roots and 5ths of the chords (creating 4th and 5th intervals), with some "double-4th" three-note voicings (two perfect 4th intervals stacked one on top of the other). This is typical for clavinet and staccato synth comping in funk styles.

Then in measures 9–16 (the sustained synth part), we are using more double-4ths, frequently inverted. For example, the A–B–E voicing on beat 1 of measure 9 is actually a B–E–A double-4th, but inverted (rearranged) to place the E on top. This B–E–A double-4th is built from the 5th of the Esus4 chord, giving us the 5th, root, and 4th of the chord respectively. Similarly, double-4ths have been built from the 2nd or 9th of the C(add9) chords, and from the 4th or 11th of the Am7 chords. Using double-4ths in this way is a great alternative to triads, if you want your synth comping to have a more hip, transparent sound.

Further Reading

For more information on funk keyboard and synth comping styles, please check out a couple of my other books: *R&B Keyboard: The Complete Guide with CD!* and *The Pop Piano Book*. For more information on all types of chord voicings, including double-4th shapes, please check out my *Contemporary Music Theory, Level Three* book. All of these books are published by Hal Leonard Corporation.

Our next synth comping example is in a pop/rock style, and again contains two different synth parts: a chordal comping part with some arpeggios in measures 1–8, and a busier arpeggiated part part in measures 9–16:

TRACK 12

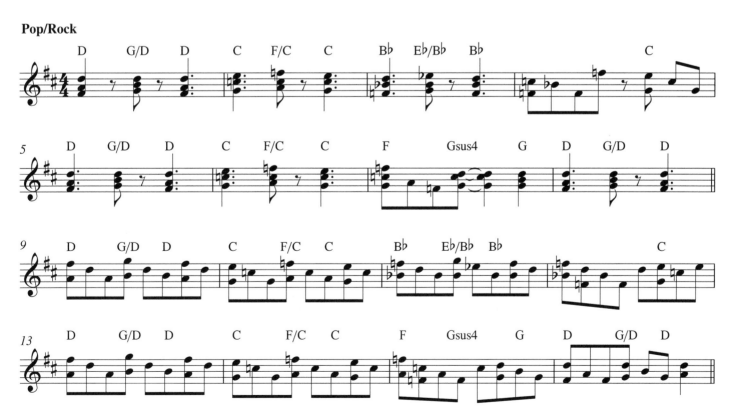

The comping synth is on the right channel, and the rest of the band is on the left channel. This time the comping synth is using the same analog brass synth throughout, from the ES2 softsynth (within Logic). This big, fat synth sound is perfectly suited to 1980s-style pop/rock. On the left channel, as well as the Scarbee bass and BFD2 drums we heard on Track 11, we now have a guitar part played using the RealStrat virtual guitar instrument from MusicLab. In my humble opinion, this is the most realistic and playable electric guitar plug-in instrument available today.

Harmony/Theory Notes

In measures 1–8, this synth part uses a common pop/rock voicing technique called alternating triads. For example, during measure 1 we move from D major to G major triad and back again: the G major triad moving back to the D major triad can be thought of as a IV–I alternating triad movement, with respect to the D in the bass. Similarly, in measure 2 the F triad moving to the C triad is a IV–I with respect to the C in the bass, and so on. In measures 9–16, these upper triads are now arpeggiated (played "broken chord" style), reinforced by two-note intervals at the points of chord change.

Further Reading

For much more information on alternating triad voicing techniques, and pop/rock comping styles, please check out my *Pop Piano Book*, published by Hal Leonard Corporation.

CONTROLLER

A **controller** is a hardware device (normally a keyboard) that generates and transmits MIDI data (see p. 73). This data can then be processed by a synthesizer or sound module to produce sound. For example, in my teaching studio in Los Angeles I have a Roland A-80 keyboard controller hooked up (via a MIDI cable) to a Kurzweil MicroPiano sound module. When my student plays the Roland A-80 keyboard, the MIDI data is transmitted to the Kurzweil MicroPiano, which produces the piano sound. (Audio cables are used to connect the Kurzweil's audio outputs to my mixer.)

Keyboard controllers may or may not contain "onboard sounds" as well. My Roland A-80 is only a controller, with no sounds included; it has to be MIDI'd to another unit (or to a computer) to produce sound. By contrast, my Roland A-90EX has an "expansion board" fitted, which gives the unit onboard sounds as well as controller capability. These days, almost all electronic keyboards have some rudimentary MIDI controller functions—at least a MIDI-out jack that can be connected to another MIDI device.

One of the earliest popular keyboard controllers was the Yamaha KX-88. Although it had the old membrane-style buttons (flush with the surface of the unit) similar to their DX7 synthesizer (see p. 36), it had a heavy keyboard action and feel that many players considered realistic, resembling a grand piano. For this reason the KX-88 is still found in a number of studios, even though its MIDI features are rather primitive by today's standards.

Earlier MIDI controller keyboards tended to be oriented toward live performance, offering weighted keyboards, splits (enabling two different sounds to be controlled, either side of a split point), layers (enabling two different sounds to layered), and other controller features. In the 21st century, although these performance controllers are still manufactured, the emphasis has shifted toward smaller, more portable keyboard controllers designed for use with computer recording setups. These smaller controllers can also have trigger pads to activate samples, drum hits, etc., and a USB output to interface with a computer. Korg's KONTROL49 is a good example of this new breed of controller:

Don't forget that a MIDI controller doesn't have to be a keyboard, though most are. Guitar players can get in on the fun with controllers such as Roland's GR-33, and saxophone players can expand their sound pallette with Akai's EWI (Electronic Wind Instrument), which has a similar action to a soprano sax.

CUBASE

Cubase is a music production and recording program, manufactured by Steinberg. It is one of the leading DAW (digital audio workstation, see p. 26) softwares currently available. Cubase runs on both Macintosh and Windows computers. Its main "arrange" page—with a vertical list of tracks, and a horizontal timeline—has influenced many other similar products:

Cubase started off as a MIDI sequencer program in the late 1980s, along with competitors at the time such as MOTU's Performer and Opcode's Vision. It was originally developed for Atari computers, before being adapted for use on Macintosh and Windows platforms. As computer power developed during the 1990s, Cubase added audio processing (recording, editing, and playback of digital audio) alongside its MIDI functions. Then in 2002 Cubase SX was introduced. This was a complete rewrite, based on Steinberg's high-end post-production software Nuendo. Cubase SX was considered a major leap forward in sound quality and functionality.

In 2006, Cubase 4 was released, with a redesigned GUI (graphical user interface), and various built-in softsynths (virtual instruments). This continued the trend of "bundling" softsynths in together with the DAW software, that we have seen from other manufacturers in the late 2000s. In 2009, Cubase 5 then upped the ante with yet more bundled softsynths and effects, and a Virtual Control Room feature to control multiple input sources and monitors. Like other modern DAWs, Cubase also has good music score creation and editing features.

For those who don't need the full power of Cubase 5, Steinberg also currently offers a scaled-down version called Cubase Studio 5, as well as an entry-level version called Cubase Essential 5. (Corporate note: In 2003, Steinberg was acquired by the U.S. company Pinnacle Systems; it was then sold to Yamaha in 2004.)

DECAY

In a synthesizer, the **decay** is the second stage of a envelope generator (see p. 41), which is a modifer normally applied to the filter (see p. 44) to control the timbre, or to the amplifier (see p. 9) to control the volume. The attack is the time taken for the envelope to move from its peak, to the sustain level (see p. 124).

In musical terms, a longer decay time applied to a (conventional low-pass) filter means that the sound will become darker more slowly after the attack peak, until the sustain level (frequency) is reached. By contrast, a shorter decay time applied to the filter means that the sustain level (frequency) occurs right after the attack peak, which may cause a more abrupt change in the timbre. A longer decay time applied to the the amplifier means that the sound will more slowly become quieter after the attack peak, until the sustain level (volume) is reached. By contrast, a shorter decay time applied to the amplifier means that the sustain level (volume) occurs right after the attack peak, which may cause a more abrupt change in the volume.

The recorded example on Track 13 demonstrates these principles, playing a single repeated note and using a simple sawtooth waveform (see p. 115) generated by the ES2 synth plug-in within Logic (see p. 67).

> The first group of four notes uses different decay times applied to the filter (with the attack time set to 730 ms in each case):
>
> - 0 ms (milliseconds), 500 ms, 1500 ms, and 3000 ms.

TRACK 13

> The second group of four notes use different decay times applied to the amplifier (with the attack time set to 1000 ms in each case):
>
> - 0 ms, 500 ms, 1500 ms, and 2000 ms.

In the first group of four notes, you hear the same attack time (i.e., the time taken for the sound to get to its maximum brightness). You can also hear that, as the decay time increases, the sound takes progressively more time (after the attack peak) to become darker, i.e., to reach the sustain level of "brightness." In the first of these examples, you can hear the timbral change very abruptly after the attack peak (as the decay time is set to zero).

In the second group of four notes, you hear the same attack time (i.e., the time taken for the sound to get to its maximum loudness). You can also hear that, as the decay time increases, the sound takes progressively more time (after the attack peak) to become quieter, i.e., to reach the sustain level of "loudness" (which in this case is zero). In the first of these examples, you can hear the sound cut out very abruptly after the attack peak (as the decay time is set to zero, and the sustain level is also zero).

DIGITAL AUDIO WORKSTATION

A **digital audio workstation (DAW)** is a piece of software running on a Mac and/or Windows PC platform that enables you to record, edit, and produce music. Many DAWs started out as MIDI sequencing programs some years ago, and then added audio recording facilities as computer processing power increased. Here are some leading examples of digital audio workstation software:

- *Cubase* (see p. 23), manufactured by Steinberg. Runs on Mac and Windows platforms. Good all-round DAW for MIDI and audio editing, now with virtual instruments included. Based on Steinberg's top-of-the-line Nuendo post-production software.

- *Digital Performer* or DP (see p. 27), manufactured by Mark of the Unicorn (MOTU). Runs on the Mac platform only. A widely used DAW (popular with touring musicians and film composers), with excellent MIDI and audio capabilities. However, the included softsynths (virtual instruments) are not as strong as some of the competition, particularly Logic Studio.

- *Garageband* (see p. 48), manufactured by Apple. Runs on Mac platform only. A stream-lined and basic DAW that Apple installs as part of the iLife suite of programs, on new Mac computers. A fun entry-level program for beginners/hobbyists.

- *Live* (see p. 67), manufactured by Ableton. Runs on Mac and Windows platforms. A loop-based DAW favored by electronic musicians and DJs. Designed from a live performance point-of-view, with a compact and easy-to-use interface.

- *Logic Studio* (see p. 67), manufactured by Apple. Runs on Mac platform only. Excellent "workflow" and ease-of-use. Top-of-the-line virtual instruments included. Aggressively priced for such a powerful software package.

- *ProTools* (see p. 100), manufactured by Digidesign. Runs on Mac and Windows platforms. The industry standard for audio recording, editing and mixing. However, the MIDI facilities are not as strong as some of the competition (e.g., Cubase or DP), the release of ProTools 8 notwithstanding.

- *Reason* (see p. 105), manufactured by Propellerhead. Runs on Mac and Windows platforms. An expandable DAW with a unique rack-style interface, favored by electronic musicians. Good softsynths included, but no capability to use third-party virtual instruments. (Reason synths can, however, be used within other DAW hosts, via the ReWire connection protocol.)

- *Sonar* (see p. 120), manufactured by Cakewalk. Runs on Windows platform only. Another good all-round DAW for MIDI and audio editing, with virtual instruments included. Sonar is the first DAW with 64-bit native processing, enabling the program to take advantage of 64-bit versions of Windows XP and Vista operating systems.

A typical recording session with a DAW and using a keyboard controller, normally involves the following steps:

1. Open up the DAW and launch (instantiate) a virtual instrument. This may be a softsynth that comes bundled with the DAW, or a third-party instrument from another manufacturer. This then generally appears as an audio or instrument track in the main arrange window of the DAW.

2. If necessary, create a MIDI track to be paired with the audio or instrument track. Some DAWs will do this for you automatically (e.g., Logic, Sonar), and in some you do this manually (e.g., DP).

3. Record-enable the MIDI track, and check that you hear the desired sound when you play the keyboard controller. Then set up the click track and countoff (if necessary), hit record on the DAW, and play the part on your keyboard. The MIDI data should now be recorded in the appropriate MIDI track.

4. Do any necessary editing/fixing of the MIDI data within the DAW.

5. Repeat steps 1–4 for other the tracks/instruments within your song arrangement.

6. When all the tracking and editing is finished, you'll switch over to the DAW's mixer page, to mix the final product to a single stereo track (or surround-sound if you prefer). Then it's done!

DIGITAL PERFORMER

Digital Performer (DP) is a music production and recording program manufactured by Mark of the Unicorn (MOTU). It is one of the leading DAW (digital audio workstation, see p. 26) softwares currently available. DP runs on the Macintosh computer platform only. Here's a screen shot of a typical "arrange" page within DP:

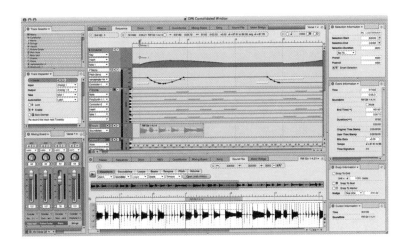

Digital Performer started off as a MIDI sequencer program (called Performer) in the 1980s, along with competitors at the time such as Steinberg's Cubase and Opcode's Vision. From this early period, Performer gained a reputation for excellent MIDI features and implementation. As computer power developed during the 1990s, Performer added audio processing (recording, editing, and playback of digital audio) alongside its MIDI functions, and was then renamed Digital Performer. At this time, it was common to use DP as a front-end application to the Audiomedia hard-disk recording system (from Digidesign), which later developed into ProTools.

In the early 2000s, the Mac community made an important transition from OS9 (operating system) to OSX. Digital Performer version 3 was the last version to run on OS9, and then version 4 was completely rewritten to run on OSX. DP version 4 was released in 2003. Then beginning with version 5, DP started to include virtual instruments in an attempt to keep up with competitors such as Apple's Logic Studio. In 2008 MOTU released DP version 6, with a redesigned user interface to improve workflow and better integration with Final Cut Pro, strengthening DP's already significant market share among film and soundtrack composers. I have used Performer and Digital Performer for nearly 20 years, and have had excellent results on a wide variety of projects.

Now we'll listen to a couple of musical examples that were created in DP. Our first is in an electronic dance style, and uses only the softsynths bundled with DP (i.e., no third-party instruments). On this example we'll spotlight the synth comping part:

TRACK 14

Electronic Dance

Listen to the track and you'll hear that the synth comping sound is on the right channel, with the rest of the band on the left channel. The synth comping is a simple single-oscillator synth produced from DP's Polysynth instrument plug-in. The instruments on the left channel are also produced from DP plug-ins: the bass is from Bassline (a monophonic analog synth), and the drums are an emulation of a Roland TR-808 drum machine, from the Model 12 drum synthesizer. Also, the rhythmic arpeggio synth you hear starting in measure 9 on the left channel is from the Modulo synth plug-in.

While these virtual instruments are fun to have within DP, I would feel somewhat limited if they were the only instruments available—i.e., if I didn't use any third-party softsynths/instruments (as opposed, say, to using Logic Studio, where it would be feasible to do many projects just with the bundled softsynths that are included). Much as I have appreciated using DP over the years, I think MOTU now has some catching up to do if it really wants to compete in this area.

Harmony/Theory Notes

Note that this synth part is contained mostly within the B minor pentatonic scale (B D E F♯ A), which is in turn built from the tonic of the minor key (B minor in this case). These two-note voicings project well, and are often more effective than playing a full chord for this type of synth part.

Our next DP example is in a dramatic/film score style, and uses third-party (non-DP) soft-synths/instruments. On this example we'll spotlight the cello ensemble part:

TRACK 15

Dramatic/Film Score

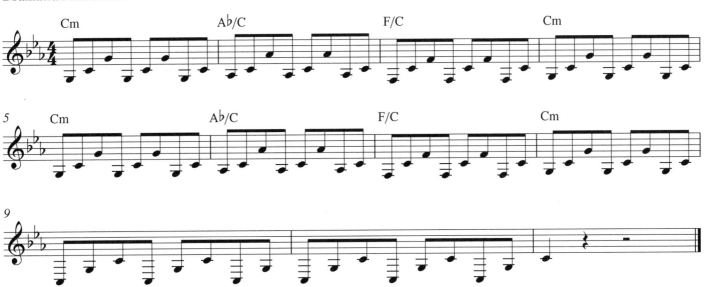

Listen to the track and you'll hear that the cello sound is on the right channel, with the remaining instruments on the left channel. The cello part uses a cello ensemble sound from the Vienna Symphonic Library (VSL) within the Kontakt 3 software sampler/synth (see p. 61). Also on the left channel the low drone note (a common device used in suspenseful movie and TV writing) is a combination of a VSL orchestral bass from Kontakt 3, and the famous "Hollywood String Section" patch from the Atmosphere/Omnisphere softsynth (see p. 14). The remaining cellos, horns, and percussion on the left channel are also from Kontakt 3.

DIGITAL SYNTHESIZER

A **digital synthesizer** uses digital signal processing (DSP) techniques to create sounds. Early digital synthesis experiments were done on mainframe computers, as a result of academic research into sound. In the 1980s digital synthesizer technology became widely available, in the form of Yamaha's wildly successful DX7 synthesizer (see p. 36). The clean, bright sound of this classic synth was a marked contrast to the other (analog) synthesizers available at the time. The earliest digital synths used simple hard-wired digital circuitry, which was then followed by high-speed microprocessors in later models.

Under the umbrella of digital synthesis, there are various synthesis methods, each of which uses microprocessors and DSP technology. Here is a quick overview of these methods:

- *Additive synthesis* (see p. 6) combines multiple harmonics (partials) to create detailed waveforms.

- *Frequency modulation* or *FM synthesis* (see p. 45) takes a simple waveform and "modulates" it with another waveform in the audio range to create complex sounds. The Yamaha DX7 is the best-known synth to use this technology.

- *Granular synthesis* (see p. 49) splits sounds into small "grains" and then re-combines them in many different ways. It's great for "soundscapes" and effects.

- *Phase distortion synthesis* (see p. 89) modifies ("distorts") the phase angle of sine waves, to create different waveforms.

- *Physical modeling synthesis* (see p. 89) uses equations and algorithms to simulate a physical instrument's characteristics (or to create a new instrument).

- *Sample-based synthesis* (see p. 112) uses digital recordings of acoustic and electronic instruments.

- *Wavetable synthesis* (see p. 139) plays different sounds (from "wavetables") in quick succession, creating complex and evolving sounds.

So you can see that the term digital synth encompasses a lot of different methods and models. As well as the Yamaha DX7, other famous digital synths include New England Digital's Synclavier (a high-end machine that uses additive, FM, and sample-based synthesis), and Ensoniq's Mirage (the first "affordable" and widely available keyboard sampler).

In this section we have two music examples using digital synthesis. First is an R&B ballad groove with an electric piano sound that uses FM or Frequency Modulation synthesis:

TRACK 16

R&B Ballad

Listen to the track and you'll hear that the electric piano is on the right channel, and the rest of the band is on the left channel. Try playing along with this example, using your favorite electric piano patch. One of the most common uses of FM synths, such as the DX7, was to provide this type of bright, bell-like electric piano sound, a staple R&B ballad ingredient in the 1980s. This electric piano example was produced using the FM8 softsynth from Native Instruments, a computer-based successor to the venerable DX7. The FM8 is also providing the "light digital synth pad" that you hear in the backing band, on the left channel.

Harmony/Theory Notes

The above electric piano part makes use of upper structure triads. For example, the right hand notes on the Bm7 chord form a D major triad (D F♯ A). These are the 3rd, 5th, and 7th of the Bm7 chord, and can be thought of as a major triad (D major in this case) built from the 3rd of the chord (Bm7 in this case). Other upper structure triads are also used in this example, as follows:

- the right hand notes on the C♯m7 chord form an E major triad (built from the 3rd of the chord)

- the right hand notes on the F♯m7 chord form an A major triad (built from the 3rd of the chord)

- the right hand notes on the Dmaj7 chord form an F♯ minor triad (built from the 3rd of the chord)

- the right hand notes on the E11 chord form a D major triad (built from the 7th of the chord)

Also, the Amaj9 chords make use of an upper structure four-part chord: the right hand notes form a C♯m7 four-part chord, which is built from the 3rd of the Amaj9 chord.

Further Reading

For much more information on R&B keyboard and synth comping styles, please check out a couple of my other books: *R&B Keyboard: The Complete Guide with CD!* and *The Pop Piano Book*. Both of these books are published by Hal Leonard Corporation.

Next up is a synth-pop example using a sampled horn sound. Sampled instruments use actual recordings ("samples") of real instruments, for greater realism:

TRACK 17

Synth-pop

Listen to the track and you'll hear that the horn "stabs" are on the right channel and the rest of the band is on the left channel. The horns in this example were produced using the EXS24 sample-based synth (within Logic). In the backing band, the FM8 softsynth is helping out again, providing the pulsating eighth-note synth comping, as well as the hard-edged synth bass (another typical FM-type sound).

Harmony/Theory Notes

Notice that the horn lines are mostly contained within the F♯ minor pentatonic scale (F♯ A B C♯ E), which is built from the tonic of the minor key (F♯ minor in this case). This is a common technique in minor-key pop and R&B songs. Also, the horns are using an arranging technique known as "one-part density," which means that only one pitch is sounding at one time (in octaves). For the majority of pop applications, your synth horn parts will sound more realistic with one-part density, as opposed to playing thicker chords.

DRUM AND BASS

Drum and Bass is an electronic dance music style, also known as **jungle**, that emerged in the early 1990s. The term "drum and bass" is often abbreviated to "D&B" or "DnB." This style typically uses "broken beat" drums at fast tempos (usually 155–180 beats per minute) and heavy bass lines that are sometimes quite complex. Although the drums and bass are not the only instruments used in this style, they are by far the most important and they are usually to the forefront in a D&B mix. The style heavily features both sampled and synthesized bass sounds, and classic drum machines such as Roland's TR-808.

Now we'll look at a couple of drum and bass examples, and spotlight the synth bass part on each. Our first example was created in Logic (see p. 67), using Logic's internal sounds and plug-ins:

TRACK 18

Drum and Bass

Listen to the track and you'll hear that the synth bass is on the right channel, with the other instruments on the left channel. The bass has a hollow quality, typical of an analog synth using a square waveform (see p. 122). On the second repeat, a "gated" synth part is added on the left channel, from the ES2 synth plug-in within Logic. This part is synced to the tempo of the track, a common effect in electronic dance music styles.

Harmony/Theory Notes

Note that the above bass line is derived from a C blues scale (C E♭ F G♭ G B♭). There is normally not much harmony at work in drum and bass styles; however, the simple root-and-5th synth voicings on the second repeat, together with the bass line, are implying the chord symbols shown.

The next drum and bass example was created in Reason (see p. 105), using Reason's internal sounds and plug-ins:

TRACK 19

Drum and Bass

Listen to the track and you'll again hear that the synth bass is on the right channel, with the other instruments on the left channel. This time the synth bass is produced using Thor, a noted plug-in synth within Reason, with some extra bite due to resonance (see p. 108) being applied to the filter. The synth comping that starts in measure 9 on the left channel is also produced from Thor.

DRUM MACHINE

A **drum machine** is an electronic musical instrument that produces drum sounds and rhythmic patterns. Early commercially available drum machines used analog synthesis, rather than samples of real drums and percussion, to create the drum sounds. These machines were therefore not particularly realistic, although they each had an individual sonic character. Notable among these early models were the Roland CR-78 (one of the first programmable rhythm machines), and the more affordable Boss "Doctor Rhythm" DR-55.

Then in 1980 the Linn LM-1 drum machine was introduced. This was the first drum machine to use digital samples (i.e., real recordings) of drums. The LM-1 caused an immediate sensation, and was used on numerous hit records from the 1980s, notably by Human League, Prince, Gary Numan, and many others. I still remember the *Keyboard Magazine* ad for this unit at the time, which simply said "Real Drums." A lower-cost version of the Linn drum machine was released in 1982, this time including a crash cymbal sample that was not implemented in the original LM-1 due to memory limitations.

Older-style analog drum machines were still being produced in the early 1980s, including the Roland TR-808 and TR-909 models. Ironically, these machines were overlooked at first, as they were less popular than digital machines such as the LM-1. However, starting in the late 1980s and continuing into the 1990s, these machines became very popular within the fast-growing hip hop and electronic dance music community. Although these drum machines were discontinued by the mid-1980s, their sounds have been sampled endlessly, and have been used on a great many recordings up until the present time.

Aside from their association with particular music styles/eras, drum machines are also very convenient as a practice, teaching, and rehearsal tool. Perhaps the most popular unit of this type is the Alesis SR-16, introduced in 1991 and still being manufactured in the late 2000s.

The SR-16, like similar competitors from Roland/Boss and Korg, contains a number of pre-programmed rhythm patterns or presets, together with drum pads that can be used to trigger sounds. I have had one in my home studio in Los Angeles for many years, and I still use it when teaching lessons. Now we'll look at a music example in a funk style, using an SR-16 preset rhythm pattern ("Funk 2") as part of the rhythm section on the left channel. The featured instrument on this track is a "modeled" clavinet sound:

TRACK 20

Funk

Listen to the track and you'll hear that the clavinet is on the right channel, and the rest of the band, including the SR-16 drum pattern, is on the left channel. The clavinet sound is created with physical modeling (see p. 89), using the EVD6 "modeled" clavinet softsynth within Logic. The backing band on the left channel also includes the Scarbee Red Bass virtual instrument, and an organ pad from the Native Instruments B4 plug-in during the last four measures.

Harmony/Theory Notes

Note that the above clavinet part is derived mainly from the roots and 5ths of the various chords, creating perfect 4th and 5th interval voicings. This technique is well-suited to the staccato sound of the clavinet, and is commonly used in R&B/funk comping grooves.

DX7

The **Yamaha DX7** is one of the most famous and best-selling synthesizers of all time. It uses frequency modulation (FM) synthesis (see p. 45), a method made possible by the advances in digital signal processing (DSP) technology in the 1980s. The DX7 was the first commercially successful digital synthesizer (see p. 29). Its clean, bright sound was a big contrast to the analog synthesizers available at the time. It was particularly good at creating electric pianos, bells, and other metallic sounds, and was heard on innumerable pop records throughout the 1980s.

The first DX7s were manufactured in 1983 and did not have a full MIDI implementation, as MIDI was in its infancy at the time and the full MIDI specifications had not been completed. However, by 1987 when the DX7 II series and the DX7S were released, the MIDI implementation and various other features had been improved. I remember using a DX7S on gigs in Los Angeles during the late 1980s, and it was a useful part of the working keyboardist's rig at that time. Although Yamaha discontinued the DX7 series in 1989, FM synthesis lives on in various forms, including softsynths such as the well-known FM8 from Native Instruments.

Now we'll look at a couple of music examples using DX7-type sounds. Our first uses a pop-rock style, featuring a lead synth sound typical of the DX7 and of FM-style synthesis:

TRACK 21

Pop/Rock

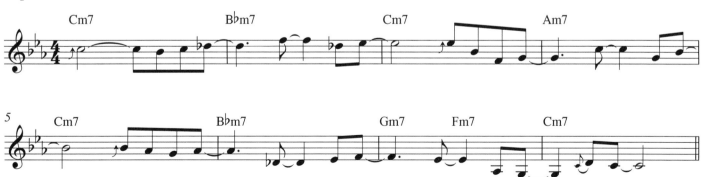

Listen to the track and you'll hear that the synth lead is on the right channel, and the rest of the band is on the left channel. The lead synth sound was produced using the FM8 softsynth from Native Instruments. This sound has a bright, metallic quality with high harmonics, and is reminiscent of the old DX7. Notice that some pitch bend (see p. 92) is being used in this lead synth part, indicated by the curved lines leading into some of the notes on the staff. Here the pitch bend wheel is pulled back before the note is played, and then allowed to return to its center position, raising the pitch to the correct level. The exception is in measure 15, where the pitch is bent up a half-step (from G up to A♭) and then back again.

The backing band on the left channel includes the Scarbee Red Bass virtual instrument, the BFD2 virtual drum instrument, the RealStrat virtual guitar instrument, and a "modeled" Rhodes electric piano from the EVP88 softsynth within Logic. Both the guitar and the bass are going through virtual amplifier simulators ("amp-sims" for short) created by IK Multimedia. RealStrat is going through the Amplitube 2 guitar amp-sim, and the Scarbee Red Bass is going through the Ampeg SVT bass amp-sim.

Harmony/Theory Notes

Note how this synth solo is organized around a "target note" approach—i.e., a specific target note (chord function) is used for each measure. For example, we go from the root of the Cm7 chord (C) in measure 1, to the 3rd of the B♭m7 chord (D♭) in measure 2, to the 3rd of the Cm7 chord (E♭) in measure 3, and so on. This gives the solo some structure, and we can then fill in between with appropriate chord and/or scale tones. In the busier section beginning in measure 9, note that we are using pentatonic scale runs to connect between the target notes. For example, the 16th notes in measure 9 are derived from the C minor pentatonic scale, the 16th notes in measure 10 are from the B♭ minor pentatonic scale, and so on. See p. 65 for more information on synth soloing.

Our next example is in a New Age style, and features a bell sound typical of the DX7:

TRACK 22

New Age

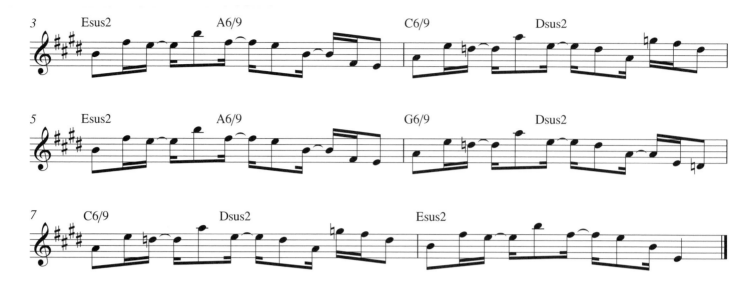

Listen to the track and you'll hear that the synth bells are on the right channel, and the other instruments are on the left channel. The bell sound was produced using the FM8 softsynth. On the left channel, we have the "Italian Grand" piano from the Ivory virtual instrument (see p. 56), as well as a soft string pad from the Absynth softsynth (from Native Instruments).

Harmony/Theory Notes

Note how this synth bell line is created using inversions of double-4th shapes (using two consective 4th intervals). For example, the first measure takes the double-4th shape F♯-B-E, and then inverts and rearranges it to go over the Esus2 and A69 chords. As we have already seen, double-4ths and their inversions are a very effective contemporary voicing technique.

Further Reading

For more information on keyboard voicing techniques including double-4ths, please check out a couple of my other books: *Smooth Jazz: The Complete Guide with CD!* and *The Pop Piano Book*. Both of these books are published by Hal Leonard Corporation.

EFFECTS

An **effect** is a treatment or manipulation applied to a sound that modifies its characteristics. Effects can be applied to keyboard synthesizers and softsynths, as well as other instruments such as guitar, bass, drums, and so on. Effects were first widely available with the use of effects pedals or "stomp boxes" for live performance, and larger rack-mounted units for recording applications. Then by the late 1980s, effects capability was added to the digital synthesizers of the time, notably including the Korg M1 workstation keyboard (see p. 72). Into the 21st century, there are many hardware and software products providing effects capability, such as:

- Modern-day effects pedals and stomp boxes made by Roland/Boss, Korg, Zoom, et al.

- Rack-mount studio units made by Lexicon, Eventide, TC Electronic, et al.

- Workstation keyboards made by Korg, Yamaha, Roland, et al.

- Digital Audio Workstations (software programs) including Cubase, Logic, Digital Performer, etc.

- Softsynths/virtual instruments including SampleTank, Kontakt, Ivory, etc.

- Dedicated software effects plug-ins made by IK Multimedia, Sonnox, AudioEase, et al.

- Amplifier simulators ("amp-sims") made by Native Instruments, IK Multimedia, Waves, et al.

Here is a brief summary of some commonly used audio effects:

- *Reverb* is the simulation of sound being produced in an enclosed space, reflecting off of the surfaces and then blending together. This is perceived as adding space and depth to the sound. The latest trend is to add convolution reverb to workstations and softsynths, which enables different room characteristics to be "modeled" with great accuracy and realism.

- *Chorus* blends a slightly delayed and pitch-shifted signal with the original. This is perceived as adding warmth and "sweetening" the sound. The delay time is short, so that it is not perceived as echo.

- *Flanging* also blends a delayed signal with the original, this time using a continuously variable delay time. This is a DSP (digital signal processing) re-creation of how flanging used to be done, by using two synchronized tape players and pressing the "flange" of one of the players, so that it would fall out of phase with the other. Flanging can be an intense effect, sometimes perceived as having a jet plane or "whooshing" sonic characteristic.

- *Phasing* splits the signal into two parts, and applies an "all-pass" filter to one of them that alters the phase. This is then recombined with the original signal. Phasing is a similar effect to flanging, and was originally created using tape machines. Phasing produces a filter-sweep type of effect, and is often perceived as giving an artificial, otherworldly character to the sound.

- *Delay* (or *echo*) adds one or more delayed signals to the original. To be perceived as delay rather than reverb, the delay time has to be around 50 milliseconds or more. Delay can be used to add a dense or ethereal quality to both acoustic and electronic instruments.

- *Overdrive* (or *distortion*) amplifies the signal past the limits of the amplifier, resulting in audio clipping. This is perceived as adding warmth or "fuzziness," particularly to electric guitar sounds.

Now we'll listen to an analog synthesizer repeating the same part through some of these effects:

TRACK 23

Listen to the track and you'll hear the same synth line repeated, as follows:

- 1st time: No effects

- 2nd time: With reverb

- 3rd time: With chorus

- 4th time: With flanging

- 5th time: With delay

The featured instrument is an analog synthesizer sound from the Absynth softsynth, from Native Instruments. The reverb effect is courtesy of IK Multimedia's Classik Studio Reverb plug-in, and the other effects (chorus, flanging, and delay) were internally applied within the DAW (in this case Logic). The delay was synced to the tempo of the track, and was set to a 16th note—i.e., the delayed signal comes in a 16th note after the original signal.

ELECTRONIC MUSIC

Electronic music is an umbrella term for music styles based on electronic instruments and technology (synthesizers, drum machines, loops/samples, computers, etc). Although in the 21st century almost all recordings and live performances rely on electronics, the term electronic music is generally reserved for those styles that use electronics as their main focal point or inspiration.

Here is a brief summary of some of the more popular electronic music styles:

- *Drum and Bass* (see p. 32), also known as jungle, emerged in the early 1990s and uses "broken beat" drums at fast tempos, usually 155–180 beats per minute. Bass lines are normally sampled or synthesized, and can be quite complex.

- *Electro* is short for electro funk, sometimes referred to as robot hip hop. It is an electronic style of hip hop, influenced by bands such as Kraftwerk. Vocals are often mechanical-sounding and electronically processed.

- *Hip Hop* (see p. 52), also known as rap, is an urban, mid-tempo music style that first emerged in the late 1970s, using a rhythmic style of spoken-word vocals (rapping) over backing beats. Modern hip hop makes extensive use of samples and sequenced loops.

- *House* (see p. 54) is an electronic dance music style, usually using medium to fast tempos (120–135 beats per minute). House music has considerable soul, funk, and disco influences, and a more "live" or organic feel compared to other electronic styles such as techno and trance.

- *Industrial Music* is intensely mechanical, using unconventional samples, noise elements and provocative lyrics. This genre reached a peak in the 1990s, also influencing the rock and metal styles of the period.

- *Synth-pop* (see p. 125) is a genre that makes extensive use of synthesizers and drum machines, within mostly conventional pop song structures and arrangements. This style's heyday was the early- to mid-1980s, although it still remains popular today.

- *Techno* (see p. 127) is an electronic dance music style that emerged in the late 1980s. Techno uses synthesized sounds and drum loops at fast tempos (135–155 beats per minute). Techno tracks often have little or no harmonic structure when compared to other electronic styles like trance.

- *Trance* (see p. 128) is another electronic dance music style that emerged in the late 1980s. It uses repetitive synthesizer phrases and melodies at fast tempos (130–165 beats per minute) and has more of a musical form (i.e., a recognizable chord progression and arrangement) than other styles such as techno or hip hop.

- *Trip hop*, which emerged in the UK during the 1990s, is a variation of hip hop that uses a laid-back, slower beat, with a moody and "spacey" feel. Trip hop tracks often use samples taken from old vinyl jazz records.

Also, progressive rock (see p. 96), while not an electronic music style per se, makes extensive use of synthesizers alongside more traditional instruments such as guitar, bass, and drums.

ENVELOPE

An **envelope**, also referred to as an **envelope generator** or **ADSR envelope**, is a component of many synthesizers and electronic musical instruments. Its purpose is to modify some aspect of the instrument's sound, usually either the tone color (timbre) or the volume (amplitude). In the earlier analog synthesizers, the envelope was a separate circuit or physical module. With the advent of digital synthesizers, envelopes are implemented in the software of the unit (or softsynth).

When you listen to an acoustic instrument, the volume and/or timbre of each note will change over time. For example, when a note is played on a cello, it normally takes a moment for the note to reach full volume, and the note will then sustain as long as the bowing continues. By contrast, when a note is played on a guitar, the maximum volume occurs immediately after the string is plucked, and the sound then fades afterward. These volume (amplitude) characteristics can be imitated in a synthesizer by applying an envelope to the amplifier stage (see p. 9).

Also, when a note is played on a brass instrument, it normally takes a moment for the upper harmonics to emerge—sometimes referred to as the "splat" of a trumpet or trombone, for example. These timbral characteristics can be imitated in a synthesizer by applying an envelope to the filter stage (see p. 44).

The typical ADSR envelope has the following components or stages:

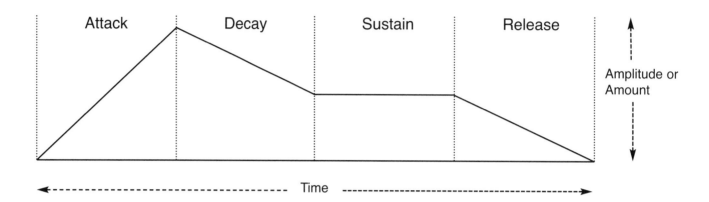

- The first stage is the *attack time* (see p. 17). This is the time taken for the envelope to reach its peak. The attack peak corresponds to the maximum volume if the envelope is applied to the amplifier, or to the maximium brightness if the envelope is applied to the filter.

- The second stage is the *decay time* (see p. 25). This is the time taken for the envelope to move from the peak to the sustain level. During this period the sound will become either quieter or darker, again depending on how the envelope is being applied.

- The third stage is the *sustain* (see p. 124). It's important to realize that this parameter is not a time period like the other stages of the envelope, but rather a level that applies as long as the note is sustained (i.e., held down on the keyboard). This value will govern the overall volume or timbre of the sound, once the attack and decay times have passed.

- The fourth stage is the *release time* (see p. 108). This is the time taken for the envelope to close, once the note has been released. This value will control how quickly the note fades away, or how quickly the brightness will change back to the level specified in the filter.

Here are a few more tips from the trenches to bear in mind when you're next programming the envelopes in your favorite keyboard or softsynth:

- For many sounds, you'll want to apply envelopes to both the filter and amplifier stages. Most modern-day synths allow you to do this. Don't forget that there's an interaction between these two envelopes—for example, if you're not hearing the effect of your filter envelope, it could be because your amplifier envelope is not letting the sound through (i.e., if the sustain level is too low).

- You'll also want to control the degree to which your envelope will modify the filter. This is variously referred to as "envelope intensity," "envelope amount," etc. on different synths. So again, if you're not hearing the effect of your filter envelope, you may need to adjust this intensity parameter.

- When an envelope is modifying the filter, the "baseline" frequency, equivalent to the bottom horizontal line on our diagram, is set by the filter cutoff parameter (see p. 44).

So to get the best results from your filter envelope, you may need to adjust the cutoff. In general, the lower the filter cutoff, the more room the filter envelope has to work with, meaning that you will hear a greater timbral difference as the envelope is applied.

Now we'll hear two examples of envelopes being applied to synthesizer sounds, both using a simple series of whole notes:

TRACK 24

Listen to Track 24 to hear a filter envelope applied to a synth brass sound. The filter opens to a peak brightness (during an attack time of 870 milliseconds) before reducing brightness (during a decay time of 440 ms) down to the sustain level.

TRACK 25

Listen to Track 25 to hear an amplifier envelope applied to a synth string sound. The amplifier builds to the peak loudness (during an attack time of 1400 ms) before reducing volume (during a decay time of 1200 ms) down to the sustain level.

Both of these synth brass and string sounds were produced from the ES2 softsynth within Logic. ES2 is a great softsynth to use for practising your envelope programming, as the GUI (graphical user interface) is very well laid out and easy to use.

FANTOM

The **Roland Fantom** is one of the most popular workstation-style keyboards in the late 2000s, alongside similarly priced competitors such as Yamaha's Motif (see p. 80), and Korg's M3 series. These machines all have a great selection of onboard sounds, multiple effects (see p. 39), and multitrack sequencing/recording capability. The Fantom series currently consists of the flagship G8 model (88 weighted keys) and the smaller G7 (76 unweighted keys) and G6 (61 unweighted keys) models.

A particular highlight of the Fantom series is the large, mouse-driven display, which makes sequencing and editing somewhat easier, particularly if you are used to doing these tasks on a computer. The onboard sounds can be supplemented via Roland's ARX expansion cards. The Fantom has 16 pads, which—in addition to triggering drum sounds and samples—can be used to jump to edit pages, enter patch numbers, and more. There are many controllers on the unit, including eight sliders, four knobs, and even a D-Beam interface that can control sound via hand movements interacting with a light beam.

FILTER

In the synthesizer world, the **filter** is the component that controls the timbre (tone color) of the sound. Filters are either low-pass (eliminating the higher frequencies above the filter cut-off point), high-pass (eliminating the lower frequencies below the filter cut-off point), or band-pass (eliminating the frequencies outside a specified band or range). Of these, the low-pass filter is by far the most commonly used.

Another important factor is the slope of the filter, which is the rate the frequencies are attenuated (reduced) after the cut-off point, expressed in "decibels per octave." Typical slopes for synthesizer filters are either 6, 12, or 24 dB per octave. (The higher the slope number, the more sharply the frequencies are reduced after the cut-off point.)

In basic analog synthesis (see p. 10), the filter stage is the second of the three main sound components, following the oscillator (see p. 86) and preceding the amplifier (see p. 9). The components in early synthesizers were voltage-controlled, so the filter stage was referred to as a voltage-controlled filter (VCF) in classic analog synthesizers. However, with the advent of digital synthesis (see p. 29), these synthesizer functions were re-created digitally, and the term "digitally controlled filter" (DCF) was then used by some synth manufacturers.

The filter stage in a synthesizer can be controlled by two important modifiers: the envelope (see p. 41) and the low-frequency oscillator (LFO, see p. 71). When an envelope is applied to the filter stage, the tone color of each note changes over time according to how the envelope is programmed. For example, a synth brass sound might have a longer attack time (see p. 17) programmed in the filter envelope, so that the upper harmonics of the sound take a moment to build when the note is played.

When a low-frequency oscillator (or LFO) is applied to the filter stage in a synthesizer, a cyclical variation in timbre occurs over time, depending on the waveform and speed of the LFO, and the degree (intensity) to which this is then applied to the filter. A typical application of this technique is to produce a wah-wah effect.

Now we'll listen to an analog synthesizer repeating the same line, with different filtering applied each time:

TRACK 26

Listen to the track and you'll hear the same synth line repeated, as follows:

- 1st time: No filtering applied. The full sawtooth waveform, with all frequencies present.

- 2nd time: Low-pass filtering applied. Note how the sound becomes darker, as the higher frequencies have been attenuated.

- 3rd time: High-pass filtering applied. Note how the sound becomes tinny and narrow, as the lower frequencies have been attenuated.

This analog synth sawtooth waveform was again produced from the ES2 softsynth within Logic.

FREQUENCY MODULATION (FM)

Frequency Modulation (FM) is a method of synthesis where the tone color of a simple waveform (see p. 138) is frequency modulated by another oscillator in the audio range. This results in complex sounds with multiple harmonics present. In FM-speak, the oscillator being modulated is known as the carrier, while the oscillator doing the modulating is (not surprisingly!) known as the modulator.

Technical note: For synthesizing harmonic or "pitched" sounds, the modulator must have a harmonic relationship to the carrier (i.e., the frequency must be an integer multiple). However, FM is also particularly good at generating non-pitched sounds such as bells and percussion, and this is achieved by using modulator frequencies that are not integer multiples of the carrier frequency.

FM synthesis was discovered by John Chowning at Stanford University in the late 1960s, and was patented in 1975. By the 1980s FM had been licensed to Yamaha, and was the basis of their hugely successful DX7 synthesizer (see p. 36). Yamaha essentially monopolized the FM synthesizer market during the 1980s, but by the mid-1990s the original patent had expired, making FM technology available to other manufacturers. Modern-day keyboard synthesizers and softsynths often incorporate FM alongside other synthesis methods, such as subtractive, sample-based, and so on. In the 21st century, a notable softsynth using FM synthesis is FM8 from Native Instruments.

Now we'll hear some examples of FM synthesis, using the FM8 softsynth. First we have an example in a dramatic/film score style, featuring a very active, morphing "drone" sound typical of FM:

TRACK 27

Dramatic/Film Score

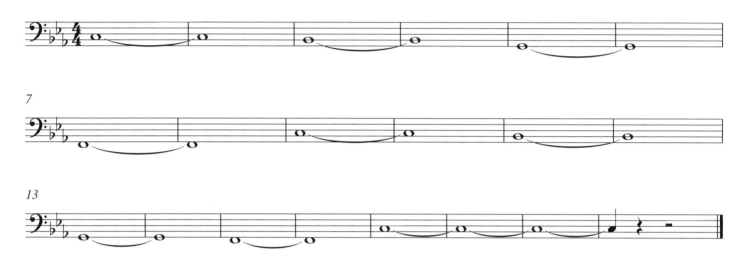

Listen to the track and you'll hear that the FM "drone" synth is on the right channel, with the other instruments on the left channel. Note that although the music part is very simple (tied whole notes), the sound imparts a lot of energy and motion to the track. On the left channel we also have an "evolving" synth texture from the Massive softsynth (again from Native Instruments), as well as some orchestral percussion courtesy of the Kontakt 3 software sampler/synth.

Our next example is in a trance style, and features a bright, staccato comping synth that is perfect for the genre:

TRACK 28

Trance

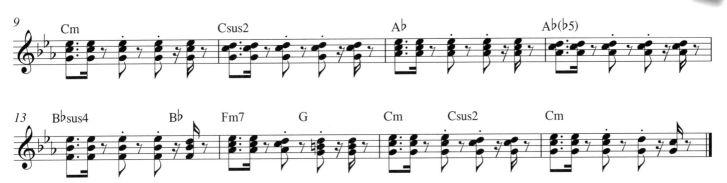

Listen to the track and you'll hear that the FM8 trance synth is on the right channel, with the rest of the band (including an analog synth bass) on the left channel.

Harmony/Theory Notes

Note how this synth part uses interior movements (resolutions) within triads. For example, the E♭ within the C minor triad in measure 1 moves to the D within the Csus2 chord in measure 2. This same note movement (E♭ to D) occurs in measures 3–4, this time between the A♭ and A♭(♭5) chords. This adds a melodic element to this trance example, and is a great way to spice up your synth parts!

GARAGEBAND

Garageband is a streamlined and basic digital audio workstation (DAW), used for music recording and production. It is manufactured by Apple and is part of the iLife suite of programs installed on all new Mac computers. Not surprisingly, Garageband runs only on the Macintosh computer platform. Here's a screen shot of a typical "arrange" page within Garageband:

Garageband was developed for Apple by Dr. Gerhard Lengeling, formerly of the German company Emagic, which Apple acquired in 2002. Emagic were the original creators of Logic (now an Apple product), and Garageband does look and feel like a stripped down version of Logic.

Although some "serious" musicians have derided Garageband, it has provided fun and enjoyment to a great many beginners and hobbyists who otherwise might not have dabbled in music sequencing and recording. It comes with a lot of pre-recorded loops in various styles, which the user can string together to make songs and arrangements. It also has some basic software instruments for recording, which can be supplemented by purchasing the optional Jam Packs available from Apple.

Garageband can import MIDI files and has piano-roll and notation-style editing, although its inability to export MIDI files is something of a limitation. It supports audio recording and playback, and has some basic effects capability. All in all, Garageband is a great entry-level program to get you started in music production if you have a recent Mac. When you outgrow it, as you probably will, I would recommend upgrading to Logic Studio (see p. 67). The interface is similar to Garageband, and Logic offers professional-level facilities at a great price!

GLIDE

Glide, also known as **portamento**, is a continuous slide between successive pitches, and has been heard on synthesizers since the progressive rock era of the 1970s, associated with Keith Emerson's playing style in particular. Of course, the ability to continuously vary the pitch between notes is not limited to the synthesizer. Unfretted stringed instruments (such as the violin), wind instruments without valves (such as the trombone), and the human voice have this capability.

Many keyboard synthesizers and softsynths have glide parameters, specifying how much glide (portamento) is required between successive notes. This effect is found in today's electronic music and progressive styles. Here's an example of glide being used on a synth lead sound, in a classic rock style:

TRACK 29

Classic Rock

Listen to the track and you'll hear the lead synth on the right channel, accompanied by an organ on the left channel. Notice that on the larger intervals (for example, the octave at the beginning of the first measure) the glide takes a little longer to reach the destination pitch. Experiment with different glide amounts applied to your lead synth sounds!

The lead synth on the right channel was produced from the ES2 softsynth within Logic, using an analog synth square wave (see p. 122). The organ sound on the left channel is from the Native Instruments B4 virtual organ instrument. These are typical sounds from the progressive and classic rock eras.

GRANULAR SYNTHESIS

Granular synthesis is a method of synthesis where waveforms or samples are split into very short pieces of up to 50 milliseconds in length. These small pieces (called "grains") can then be arranged and layered, and played back at different tempos and volume levels. The grains can be further modified by changing their duration, density, spatial position, and so on. The result is a "soundscape," sometimes referred to as a "cloud," usable for both music and sound effects. Granular synthesis can produce unique, dynamic textures that morph over time, and sound different from most other synthesis methods.

There are a number of interesting softsynths that offer granular synthesis, including Sonic Spot's Granulab, Nyrsound's Chaosynth, and LowNorth's RTGS-X. Also, the popular digital audio workstation software Reason (see p. 105) includes a softsynth called Malstrom, which the manufacturers Propellerhead call a "graintable" synth, as it combines granular and wavetable (see p. 139) synthesis methods.

Now we'll hear two music examples in an ambient electronic style, created in Reason and using the Malstrom "graintable" softsynth. Our first example features a Malstrom synth preset called "Graindrops":

TRACK 30

Ambient Electronic

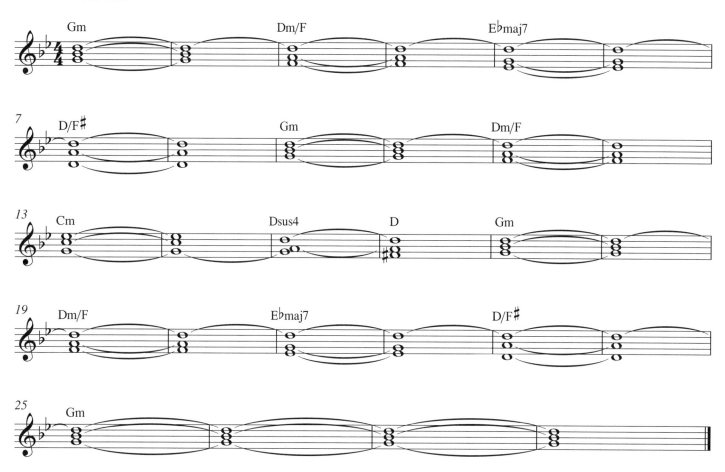

Listen to the track and you'll hear that the evolving synth pad is on the right channel, with the other instruments on the left channel, including an analog synth bass and lead synth from Thor, another great Reason softsynth.

Note that although the music part is very simple (lots of whole notes!), the sound imparts a lot of motion to the track. Our next example features another Reason synth sound called "Dystant Strings." This evolving synth is similar to the previous synth sound, but with more upper harmonics present:

TRACK 31

Ambient Electronic

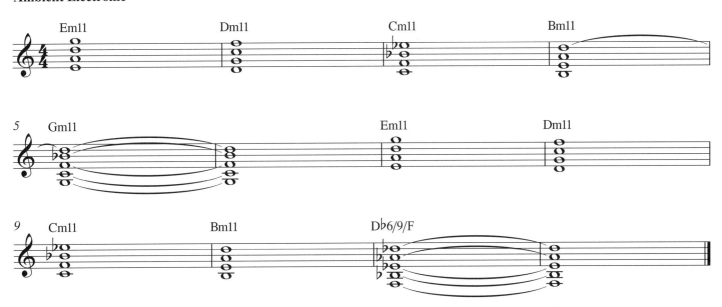

Listen to the track and you'll hear that the evolving string synth is on the right channel, with the rest of the band, again including an analog synth bass from the Thor softsynth, on the left channel.

Harmony/Theory Notes

Note how this synth part uses voicings created by stacking a series of perfect 4th intervals (or double-4th shapes that we have seen in earlier examples), creating a modern, transparent sound. These voicings are ideally suited for this particular synth texture. Also, we see that no key signature has been written, as the piece moves rapidly between different key centers due to the chords being used.

Further Reading

For more information on all types of chord voicings, including double-4th shapes, please check out my book, *Contemporary Music Theory*, *Level Three*, published by Hal Leonard Corporation.

HARMONIC

Harmonic is a term used to describe a component frequency of a sound signal. A musical sound (for example, when a guitar string is plucked) normally consists of a fundamental frequency and harmonics (overtones) that are an integer multiple of the fundamental frequency. To take a mathematical example: If x is the fundamental frequency of a sound, then the harmonics would have the frequencies 2x, 3x, 4x, and so on, in gradually decreasing proportions relative to the fundamental frequency. Relating this to musical pitches, if x in this example is the note C three octaves below middle C (sometimes referred to as C1), then the other harmonics will have the following pitches:

- 2x: one octave above (the C two octaves below middle C, or C2)

- 3x: one octave and a fifth above (the G one-and-a-half octaves below middle C, or G2)

- 4x: two octaves above (the C one octave below middle C, or C3)

- 5x: two octaves and a third above (the E nearly two octaves below middle C, or E3)

- 6x: two octaves and a fifth above (the G below middle C, or G3)

… and so on.

The presence of harmonics in addition to the fundamental, and the proportions in which they are present, determine the timbre (tone color) of the sound. Human ears have the tendency to combine harmonically related frequencies into an overall tonal impression, rather than hearing these frequencies individually.

In sounds without a specific pitch (e.g., bells, percussion), the harmonics are not exact integer multiples of the fundamental frequency. These are often referred to as inharmonics. Synthesis methods such as additive (see p. 6) and frequency modulation (see p. 45) are good at creating these types of inharmonic sounds. When multiple harmonics are present with no discernable fundamental frequency, the human ear perceives this as noise (see p. 83).

HIP HOP

Hip hop, also referred to as **rap**, is a type of music that uses a rhythmic style of speaking (rapping) over backing beats. This genre originally emerged in the 1970s, and has continued to grow and develop until the present day. Modern hip hop production makes extensive use of samplers, sequencers, synthesizers, and drum machines. The main unifying element of this style is the drum groove (loop), which is then accompanied by a bass line and other sampled or sequenced instrumental parts.

Hip hop tracks are often structurally basic, for example taking a simple two-measure phrase and repeating it for the duration of the song. However, modern hip hop sometimes features melodic, "song form" elements. Most hip hop tracks use medium tempos, typically around 90–100 beats per minute. Samples are frequently taken from old vinyl records and used in hip hop songs, which can be controversial and involve various "sample clearance" and legal issues. Hip hop production values have also blended with other styles, notably with soul and R&B to create neo-soul in the 21st century.

Now we'll look at a couple of hip hop instrumental examples, and spotlight the synth bass part on each. Our first is in a jazzy hip hop style (think Black Eyed Peas) and was created in Logic (see p. 67), using its internal sounds and plug-ins:

TRACK 32

Jazzy Hip Hop

Listen to the track and you'll hear that the synth bass is on the right channel, with the other instruments on the left channel. This example has a 16th-note subdivision; in other words, the smallest rhythmic subdivision used is a 16th-note. The synth bass has a pronounced low end (typical of hip hop styles), and a short, punchy attack. Filling out the sound on the left channel is a "modeled" electric piano with some phasing, tremolo, and a little distortion added.

The next example is in an abstract hip hop style and was created in Reason (see p. 105), using its internal sounds and plug-ins:

TRACK 33

Abstract Hip Hop

Listen to the track and you'll again hear that the synth bass is on the right channel, with the other instruments on the left channel. This time the synth bass is produced by Subtractor (an analog softsynth within Reason), using a sawtooth wave and a fairly low filter cut-off. The synth figure on the left channel is courtesy of the Thor softsynth, with a tempo-synced delay effect (see p. 40) added. Like the previous example, this one uses a 16th-note subdivision, but with a swing-16ths feel quite common in hip hop styles.

HOUSE

House is an electronic dance music style that emerged in the 1980s, with significant soul, funk, and disco influences. House music is normally at medium to fast tempos (120–135 beats per minute) and borrows disco's use of a prominent kick drum on every beat (called "four-on-the-floor"), and open hi-hat cymbals on the eighth-note offbeats. This is then accompanied by a heavy synthesized or sampled bass line. Other drums, instruments (real and/or sampled), and effects can then be added. Although house music shares some structural elements with styles such as trance and techno, it generally has a "live" music, organic feel when compared with the synthetic sound of other electronic styles.

Let's look at a couple of instrumental house examples. Our first is in a funky, "classic house" style and was created in Logic (see p. 67), with some third-party softsynth sounds. Here we'll spotlight the synth comping part:

TRACK 34

House

Listen to the track and you'll hear that the synth comping part is on the right channel, with the other instruments on the left channel. This big, bright comping synth comes from Massive, another great Native Instruments softsynth that combines a "wavetable engine" with analog-style filtering. This is a fun track to play along with; fire up your favorite "bright polysynth" and give it a shot! On the left channel is a synth bass (also from Massive) using an analog synth square wave, and a couple of digital synth comping parts (one coming in for the last eight measures) courtesy of the FM8 frequency-modulation softsynth.

The next example is in a deeper house style and was created in Reason (see p. 105), using its internal sounds and plug-ins. Here we'll spotlight the synthesized piano comping part:

TRACK 35

House

Listen to the track and you'll again hear that the synth piano is on the right channel, with the other instruments on the left channel. This was created using the Thor softsynth within Reason, using a combination of analog and wavetable oscillators. The synth bass on the left channel is from Malstrom, another softsynth within Reason, using layered sine and sawtooth waveforms. Finally, the percussive organ part that begins in measure 9 uses the "House Organ" patch within the Subtractor softsynth.

Harmony/Theory Notes

The above synth piano part makes use of upper structure triads. For example, the right hand notes on the Cm7 chord form an E♭ major triad (E♭ G B♭). These are the 3rd, 5th, and 7th of the Cm7 chord, and can be thought of as a major triad (E♭ major in this case) built from the 3rd of the chord (Cm7 in this case). Other upper structure triads are also used in this example, as follows:

- the right hand notes on the Gm7 chord form a B♭ major triad (built from the 3rd of the chord)

- the right hand notes on the Fm7 chord form an A♭ major triad (built from the 3rd of the chord)

- the right hand notes on the Dm7 chord form an F major triad (built from the 3rd of the chord)

- the right hand notes on the G11 chord form an F major triad (built from the 7th of the chord)

IVORY

Ivory is a software piano manufactured by Synthogy. It works as a plug-in within all major digital audio workstations (DAWs, see p. 26), or as a stand-alone application on your desktop or laptop computer. It also works great on rack-mount, gig-friendly computers such as the Muse Receptor.

An important technical threshold was reached with the release of Ivory in 2005. For the first time, truly realistic performances and recordings of grand pianos could be made using a MIDI keyboard controller and a computer. At the time, Ivory included samples of Steinway D, Bösendorfer Imperial 290, and Yamaha C7 grand pianos. Synthogy later introduced an "Italian Grand" (a Fazioli 308) as an add-on to the software. Each piano has individual samples for each note (at multiple velocity levels), and sophisticated controls for sound-board and sustain resonance.

Recently the software piano market became more crowded, and Ivory now has some serious competition. Its two most notable competitors are East West Quantum Leap Pianos and the Garritan Authorized Steinway. The East West product has by far the biggest sample library size (over 250GB!), and some great realism details like separately loadable samples for notes with and without sustain pedal. The Garritan product features only the Steinway piano, and (with Steinway's help) it sounds extremely authentic. Despite these other great products, Ivory is still the software piano of choice for many players and writers, due to its great sound and ease of use.

Now we'll look at a music example using Ivory. This is in a New Age style and uses the wonderful Fazioli 308 piano (and the "Italian Studio Grand" preset):

TRACK 36

New Age

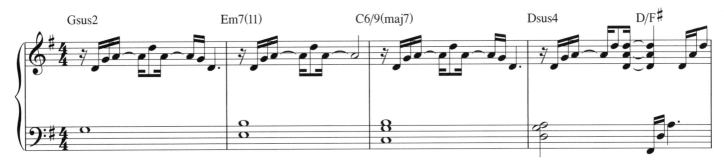

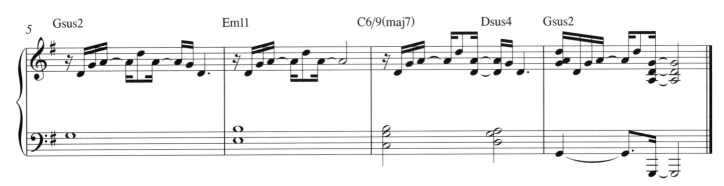

Listen to the track and you'll hear that the piano right hand (treble clef) part is on the right channel, and the left hand (bass clef) part is on the left channel.

Harmony/Theory Notes

Note how this piano part uses inversions of double-4th shapes, using two consecutive 4th intervals. The right hand plays the double-4th shape A-D-G in different inversions, and then arpeggiates these over all of the chords. Double-4th voicings are a particularly effective New Age technique.

Further Reading

For much more information on New Age styles and double-4th voicings, please check out my keyboard method *The Pop Piano Book*, published by Hal Leonard Corporation.

JUPITER-8

The **Roland Jupiter-8** is one of the most famous analog synthesizers to emerge in the early 1980s. It was an eight-voice polyphonic synth (i.e., it had the ability to sound up to eight notes at one time), and its characteristically "fat" sound was heard on many classic 1980s recordings by artists such as Duran Duran, Michael Jackson, Howard Jones, and David Bowie. Although the unit pre-dated the MIDI era, later models included Roland's DCB interface to enable it to connect with other compatible devices.

The Jupiter-8 had some advanced performance features for its time, including adjustable glide (portamento, see p. 48), a versatile arpeggiator, and performance splits (the ability to split the keyboard into two zones, with different sounds assigned to each). With the resurgence in popularity of analog synth sounds in the 1990s and beyond, the Jupiter-8 sounds are still in demand, notably for electronic dance music styles such as house and trance. In 2007 the software manufacturer Arturia introduced their Jupiter-8V softsynth, considered to be a good emulation of this classic synth. Also, the noted softsynth Atmosphere (see p. 14) includes samples of the Roland Jupiter-8, enabling it to re-create these sounds with convincing realism.

Now we'll look at a couple of music examples using Jupiter-8 sounds, derived using the Atmosphere softsynth. Our first is in a progressive rock style, featuring a lead/melody synth sound typical of the Jupiter-8:

TRACK 37

Progressive Rock

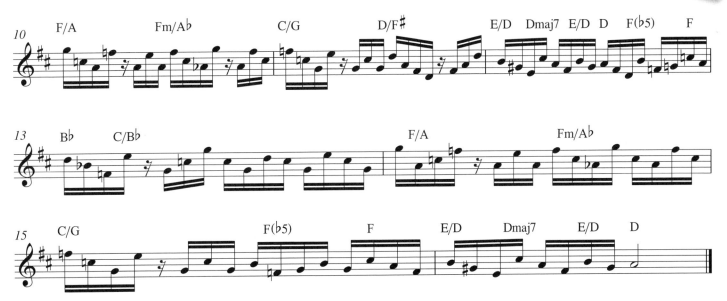

Listen to the track and you'll hear that the synth lead is on the right channel, and the rest of the band is on the left channel. The lead synth sound is using the "Sharp Bright Saws" sound within Atmosphere, based on a Jupiter-8 sample. The backing band on the left channel also includes the Scarbee Red Bass virtual instrument, the BFD2 virtual drum instrument, the Ivory virtual piano (see p. 56), and an analog synth pad from the Massive softsynth.

Harmony/Theory Notes

Note that, during the first eight measures, this synth melody/solo uses a "target note" approach, with arpeggios in between. For example, we go from the 3rd of the D chord to the 3rd of the E chord (over D in the bass) in measures 1–4, and this leads to the root of the A chord in measure 2 (over D in the bass) and measure 4 (over C# in the bass). A similar motif occurs over the C, D/C, G/C, and G/B chords in measures 5–8. From measure 9 onward, the synth part gets busier with 16th-note arpeggios, based on the upper triads within the chord symbols.

Our next example is in a pop/rock shuffle style, this time featuring a typical Jupiter-8 brass synth sound:

TRACK 38

Listen to the track and you'll hear that the brass synth comping is on the right channel, with the rest of the band on the left channel. This example uses a swing-eighths feel.

The brass synth sound is using the "Jupiter Horn Pad" sound within Atmosphere, again based on a Jupiter-8 sample. The backing band on the left channel again includes the Scarbee bass, the BFD2 drums, and the Ivory piano.

Harmony/Theory Notes

Note how this synth part uses two-note voicings with some resolutions or interior movements within the chords, during measures 1–8. Then starting in measure 9, we build up to three-note triad voicings, using an alternating triad voicing concept. For example, during measure 9 we are alternating between the D and G major triads (over D in the bass). This is a signature pop/rock keyboard sound.

Further Reading

For much more information on pop/rock keyboard styles and the use of alternating triads, please check out my keyboard method *The Pop Piano Book*, published by Hal Leonard Corporation.

KONTAKT

Kontakt is a software synthesizer and sampler manufactured by Native Instruments. It works as a plug-in within all major digital audio workstations (DAWs, see p. 26), or as a stand-alone application. Kontakt has a straightforward user interface, yet it also has deep editing and scripting features. As a result, its playback engine, known as Kontakt Player, is often licensed by different manufacturers for use with their software instruments and sample libraries. A great example of this is the Scarbee Red Bass used on various CD tracks for this book, which makes excellent use of Kontakt's advanced scripting facilities to produce a highly playable and authentic virtual bass instrument.

These third-party virtual instruments are normally bundled with a version of Kontakt Player, so that you can use them "right out of the box" even if you don't own Kontakt. When you purchase Kontakt, you basically get the Kontakt Player plus their sound content (samples). The content covers most typical sound categories: guitars, synths, basses, drums, keyboards, orchestral sounds, and so on. In this respect, Kontakt is in competition with other all-in-one softsynth samplers/workstations, such as MOTU's Mach Five and IK Multimedia's SampleTank. Kontakt version 3 now includes selections from the Vienna Symphonic Library (strings, brass, orchestral percussion, etc.). These sound great, and I have used them on various TV-scoring projects.

Now we'll look at some music examples using the sounds included in Kontakt 3. First up is an example in a rock style, and on this one we're spotlighting the synth comping/arpeggio part:

TRACK 39

Listen to the track and you'll hear that the synth comping/arpeggio part is on the right channel, with the rest of the band on the left channel. It uses an FM-style staccato synth within Kontakt. In the backing band on the left channel, we have more Kontakt instruments: a Wurlitzer A200 electric piano sample, a funk-style electric bass, and a rock drum kit.

Harmony/Theory Notes

Note that the synth part over the Cm7 chords is using 4th intervals from the C minor pentatonic scale (C E♭ F G B♭). Then on the F5 and G5 chords the synth is playing the roots and 5ths of the chords, and on the A♭, E♭, and B♭ chords the synth is playing the basic triads, with some arpeggios and resolutions. These are typical voicing solutions in pop/rock styles.

Our next example is in a dramatic/film score style, and uses some of the Vienna Symphonic Library orchestral sounds available within Kontakt 3. This time we're spotlighting the cello ensemble part:

TRACK 40

Dramatic/Film Score

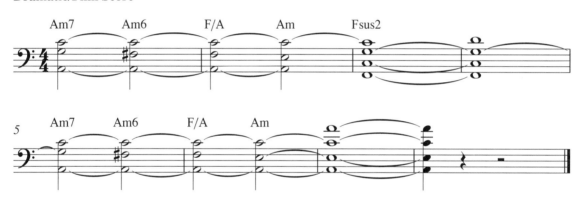

Listen to the track and you'll hear that the cello ensemble part is on the right channel, with the other instruments on the left channel. The cello sound is courtesy of the Vienna Symphonic Library within Kontakt 3. On the left channel, we have a bass ensemble drone and some timpani (again from the VSL library), as well as a flute and some light synth bells. Everything here is from Kontakt.

Harmony/Theory Notes

Note that the cello part uses three- and four-note "open" voicings, which have an overall span greater than an octave, and contain larger (4th, 5th, and 6th) intervals. Also we're using common tones (e.g., the middle C that is held on top in measures 1–3) and close voice-leading (e.g., the half-step movements G-F♯-F-E in measures 1–2). All this adds authenticity to orchestral string parts recorded with samples.

KORG

Korg is a major electronic musical instrument manufacturer that was founded in 1962. Initially focusing on electric organ products, they began manufacturing synthesizers in the 1970s. Notable among these early products were their MS-10 and MS-20, which were affordable, patchable monophonic synths. I remember playing an MS-20 in various UK rock bands in the late 1970s and early 1980s.

Then, in 1981, Korg debuted their Polysix synth, which had six-voice polyphony (i.e., it could play six notes at once), and 32 memory slots for sound programs. This was something of a price/performance breakthrough at the time, and I bought one shortly after they were introduced. Together with the MS-20 and Mono/Poly (another Korg classic from this period), the Polysix sounds are now included in Korg's Legacy Collection, a virtual synthesizer bundle that plugs into the Digital Audio Workstation (DAW) of your choice.

In 1988 Korg struck gold with the introduction of their famous M1 synthesizer/workstation (see p. 72), which offered the realism of onboard sampled sounds, in a great performance package. The early 1990s saw the introduction of Korg's Wavestation series of synths, which combined wavetable synthesis (see p. 139) with dynamic timbral control over multiple voices (also known as "vector synthesis"). The Wavestation's complex and continously evolving sounds were revolutionary at the time, and I used the Wavestation SR (rack-mount module) on various TV-scoring and music library gigs in the 1990s.

Korg has successively improved on the all-in-one keyboard synthesizer/workstation (see p. 140) since their M1 was first introduced, with the following models: 01/W (1991), X3 series (1993), Trinity and N3 series (1996), Triton (1999), and M3 series (2007). Korg also debuted their top-of-the-line Oasys workstation keyboard in 2005 (see p. 84). For those who can't afford an Oasys (that would be most musicians out there!), Korg's main contender in the synth workstation wars is their M3 series, which competes with Roland's Fantom series (see p. 44) and Yamaha's Motif series (see p. 80).

Corporate note: Shortly before Korg introduced their M1 synth in 1988, Yamaha purchased a majority of the company's stock. This was amicable, and Korg continued to compete with Yamaha in the musical instrument marketplace. Then, due in part to the phenomenal success of Korg's M1 synthesizer, they were able to buy back most of their stock from Yamaha in the early 1990s.

KURZWEIL

Kurzweil is a major electronic musical instrument manufacturer that was founded in 1982. Their first instrument was the groundbreaking K250 synthesizer, introduced in 1984. This was the very first performance instrument to have sampled sounds of acoustic instruments (brass, strings, piano, etc.) burned into the ROM (read-only memory) of the unit. Founder Raymond Kurzweil invented this instrument in consultation with Stevie Wonder, who wanted to play high-quality sampled sounds from an electronic keyboard.

The K250 paved the way for a series of high-end synthesizer workstations, beginning in 1990 with the K2000. This introduced the company's proprietary VAST (Variable Architecture Synthesis Technology) sound engine. These were great-sounding (and expensive) machines used in top recording studios and in music production for film. Then the K2500 debuted in 1996 (with increased polyphony and onboard RAM memory), followed by the K2600 in 1999. The K2600 added new effects capability, and a new "Triple Strike Piano," which was a very authentic sampled grand piano. The K2600 continued to be popular with touring musicians and studios during the 2000s, and was finally discontinued by Kurzweil in 2008.

Kurzweil introduced their PC88 keyboard in the mid-1990s. Although marketed as a keyboard controller (with weighted keys and multiple zones to control different instruments), it also had many onboard sounds and effects. This machine was much lighter (and less expensive) than the K2600, and gained a following among gigging musicians with smaller rigs. This was followed in the late 1990s by the moderately priced PC2 series of performance keyboards, containing the "Triple Strike Piano" from the K2600.

More recently there was much anticipation and excitement about the release of Kurzweil's latest generation of synthesizer workstations (their PC3 series), which hit the streets in mid-2008. The PC3 significantly improves upon the VAST synthesis method of the K2600, with new features and better sounds, including a "KB3 organ mode" with the front panel sliders functioning as drawbars.

Corporate note: Young Chang (the piano manufacturer) bought Kurzweil in 1990. Young Chang was in turn acquired by the Hyundai group of companies in 2006.

LEAD

A **synth lead** is an instrumental solo or improvisation performed on a synthesizer. In vocal music styles, a synth solo might be used to "break up" the vocal sections in a song, and to add interest and excitement (think Tina Turner's "Nutbush City Limits" or Emerson, Lake and Palmer's "Lucky Man"). Synth solos are used in many styles, from progressive rock and pop/rock to synth-pop and contemporary jazz (including smooth jazz). Synth solo timbres can range from fat analog textures (a perennial favorite), to cutting FM-style synths (common in 1980s pop), to morphing wavetable synths, and so on.

Our first synth lead example is in a synth-pop style, and features a bright FM-style lead synth courtesy of the Absynth softsynth (from Native Instruments):

TRACK 41

Synth-pop

Listen to the track and you'll hear that the synth lead is on the right channel, with the other instruments on the left channel. The lead synth has a bright, cutting quality with some inbuilt vibrato (see p. 136), and is typical of 1980s synth-pop. On the left channel, the bass and comping synths (including the tempo-synced comping part) are all produced from the ES2 softsynth within Logic.

Harmony/Theory Notes

A "target note" approach is used in this synth solo. For example, we move from the root of the Em chord (E) in measure 1, to the root of the D chord (D) in measure 2, to the 5th of the Em chord (B) in measure 3, to the root of the A chord (A) in measure 4, and so on. The connecting tones in between are from the E minor pentatonic scale (E G A B D). Then the busier section starting in measure 9 is based on arpeggios of the chord symbols, with some scalewise connecting tones added. This is varied in measure 12 with the use of an E blues scale (E G A B♭ B D) over the A major chord.

Our next synth lead example is in a pop/rock style, and features a Minimoog-style lead from the Atmosphere softsynth (see p. 14):

TRACK 42

Pop/Rock

Listen to the track and you'll again hear that the synth lead is on the right channel, with the other instruments on the left channel. This time the synth lead has a characteristically warm, analog quality, with a small amount of glide (see p. 48) added between the notes. The backing band on the left channel features an all-star virtual instrument line-up: BFD2 virtual drums, Scarbee virtual bass, RealStrat virtual guitar, Ivory virtual piano, and an analog synth comp from the Massive softsynth.

Harmony/Theory Notes

Again we see a "target note" approach in this synth solo as we move from the 3rd of the Dm chord, to the root of the G chord (inverted over B in the bass), to the 3rd of the C chord, and so on. The busier section starting in measure 9 is based on arpeggios of the chords, with pentatonic scale tones added.

LIVE

Live is a loop-based music production and recording program, manufactured by Ableton. Unlike most other DAW (digital audio workstation, see p. 26) softwares currently available, Live is designed from a performance point-of-view, with a compact interface and the ability to record, edit, and manipulate tracks—all in real time. Live runs on both Macintosh and Windows computers, and is particularly favored by electronic musicians and DJs. Here's a screen shot of the main "arrange" page within Live:

Live was first released in 2001 and is currently up to version 7. The latest version features "elastic audio," enabling users to match different samples and audio files with the loops currently running. This is very useful for DJing and re-mixing projects, and can also be used to match music to picture or vice versa. Live ships with two built-in instruments: Impulse is a drum synthesizer/sequencer, and Simpler is a basic sampler. Additional software instruments (synths, samplers, and drum machines) are available by purchasing the Ableton Suite.

For those not needing the full power of Live 7, Ableton also currently offers a scaled-down version called Live 7 LE that has fewer audio inputs and effects than the full version, and does not offer software connectivity via ReWire.

LOGIC STUDIO

Logic Studio is a suite of programs containing Logic Pro, a leading music production and recording program manufactured by Apple. Logic Pro is one of the leading DAW (digital audio workstation, see p. 26) softwares currently available. The current version of Logic runs on the Macintosh computer platform only. Here's a screen shot of a typical "arrange" page within Logic:

Logic was originally created by the German company Emagic, and was popular among both Mac and PC users from the early 1990s. Around this time, in a similar fashion to competitor DAWs such as Cubase and Digital Performer, Logic added the ability to record and mix audio tracks alongside MIDI tracks. By the early 2000s, Logic was up to version 6 and had acquired a more streamlined user interface, and various built-in softsynths and audio processing plug-ins.

Emagic was acquired by Apple in 2002, and Logic became a Mac-only program soon afterward. In 2004 Apple released version 7 of the software, renamed Logic Pro. This version consolidated many different products originating from Emagic, including more instrument and effects plug-ins, and also added ProTools TDM support. Around this time Apple debuted a scaled-down version called Logic Express, and introduced an entry-level derivative called Garageband (see p. 48) that was included on new Mac computers as part of the iLife suite of programs.

In late 2007 Apple released the Logic Studio suite, including version 8 of Logic Pro (now no longer sold as a separate product, only as part of Logic Studio). Logic Pro currently includes some great softsynths, including ES2 (an analog and wavetable synthesizer), Sculpture (a physical modeling synth), and Ultrabeat (a drum synthesizer and step sequencer, see p. 134), to name a few. Although several DAWs claim to be self-contained all-in-one production suites, Logic actually delivers in this area, as the included softsynths and plug-ins are top-notch. This, together with its ease-of-use and affordability, makes it the DAW to beat.

Now we'll listen to a couple of musical examples that were created in Logic, and use only the included softsynths (i.e., no third-party instruments). Our first example is in an R&B/funk style, and here we'll spotlight the staccato synth part:

TRACK 43

R&B/Funk

Listen to the track and you'll hear that the synth sound is on the right channel, with the remaining instruments on the left channel. This is a metallic-sounding staccato synth from the ES2 softsynth within Logic. The backing band on the left channel is also all Logic virtual instruments: the electric piano is a "modeled" Rhodes Mk II piano from the EVP88 softsynth, the synth bass is from the EXS24 software sampler, and the drum groove is using the "Studio Tight Kit" from the Ultrabeat drum softsynth.

Harmony/Theory Notes

This synth part is created from minor pentatonic scales, built from the root of each chord. For example, the figure in measures 1–2 is derived from the E minor pentatonic scale (E G A B D) built from the root of the E7sus4 chord. Similarly, the figure in measures 3–4 is derived from the F minor pentatonic scale (F A♭ B♭ C E♭), and so on. In measures 1–8 the figure alternates between fourth intervals (i.e., the A-D and B-E intervals in measures 1–2) and single notes, most often the root of the chord. Then in measure 9–16 the single-note figure continues with a lot of 16th-note upbeats or anticipations. This is common in busier funk and fusion styles.

Our next example is in a pop/rock style and features a synth brass comping part:

TRACK 44

Pop/Rock

Listen to the track and you'll hear that the synth brass sound is on the right channel, and the rest of the band is on the left channel. The brass synth uses the "Classic Synth Brass" preset within the ES2 softsynth. The backing band on the left channel includes a "modeled" clavinet from the EVD6 softsynth, and the "Fingered Bass" sample from the EXS24 software sampler.

Harmony/Theory Notes

This synth part is mostly created from triads, with some interior resolutions within chords. For example, in measure 3 on the C(add9) chord, the 9th (D) moves to the 3rd (E). Similarly, in measure 4 on the D chord, the 4th (G) moves to the 3rd (F#). This type of motion adds interest to the part, and is typical of the more "evolved" pop/rock that emerged in the 1980s.

LOOP

In the electronic music world, a **loop** is musical passage or sample that is repeated. These days, looping is most typically achieved using digital audio workstation (DAW) computer software (see p. 26). In particular, DAWs such as Ableton Live (see p. 67) and Reason (see p. 105) are oriented toward working with loops, and are therefore favored by musicians working in electronic music styles such as techno, drum and bass, and hip hop. However, other more traditional DAWs such as Cubase and Digital Performer also have the capability to loop MIDI and audio tracks, even though they are geared toward working with conventional song structures/arrangements.

Drum and percussion tracks (acoustic and/or electronic) constitute the most typical application of looping in today's styles. For example, a musician may use a pre-existing drum loop as a starting point for a demo or composition. This loop may come from a sample or loop library, or it may be available within the DAW being used. DAWs such as Garageband, Logic Studio, and Reason come with a generous selection of loops for this purpose. Phrases played on other musical instruments (bass, keyboard/synth, guitar, etc.) can be looped in the same manner.

A loop can be used as part of a sample in a musical instrument. For example, an instrument sample with a long sustain (such as an organ) might have the sustain portion looped on playback, rather than using a long sample of the overall sound including the sustained portion. This is more efficient, as it saves on computer memory and processing resources. Early sample-playback workstation synths such as Korg's M1 (see p. 72) and Roland's D50 made use of this technology, by combining an "attack" sample (i.e., the beginning of the sound) with the sustained part of the sound (i.e., a looped sample).

LOW-FREQUENCY OSCILLATOR

A **low-frequency oscillator (LFO)** is a control signal that is below the range of human hearing (i.e., the frequency is lower than 20 Hz). In a synthesizer, this can then be used to modulate or vary the audio signal, creating a variety of effects, including tremolo (see p. 131) and vibrato (see p. 136). Like oscillators within the audio range, the LFO is normally a periodic waveform such as a sawtooth, sine, square, or triangle wave. (See individual entries for these waveforms.)

Low-frequency oscillators first appeared on modular synths in the 1960s and 1970s and on the early all-in-one analog synths of the 1970s. Since then LFOs have been incorporated on most synths up until the present day, including the latest generation of samplers and soft-synths.

As well as the more typical tremolo and vibrato effects, there are various other applications for LFOs. For example, the LFO can be used to modulate a filter cut-off frequency. This can create a wah-wah effect, or (at very slow LFO speeds) can cause the sound to become gradually darker or brighter over time. When combined with resonance (see p. 108), LFO modulation of the cut-off frequency can produce dramatic "filter sweep" effects. An LFO might also be used to control the tempo of an arpeggiator (see p. 13) on a synthesizer.

Technical note: On Korg synthesizers, the LFO is often referred to as a Modulation Generator (or MG).

M1

The **Korg M1** is the best-selling digital keyboard of all time, and the best-known workstation keyboard, combining sound generation and sequencing capabilities (see p. 116). From its release in 1988 until it was discontinued six years later, more than 250,000 units were sold. The M1 was a 16-voice polyphonic synthesizer (reducing to eight voices when using dual-oscillator programs), and it set new standards for other synthesizer manufacturers.

The big news about the M1 was that it included samples of real acoustic instruments (piano, bass, guitar, etc.). These were typically used for the attack part of the sound, with the sustain part coming from synthesized waveforms. These were then passed through filter and amplifier sections, and an independent effects section including reverb, delay, flanger, and chorus. The sampled waveforms (although basic by today's standards), together with the onboard effects, gave the M1 a depth and realism that was revolutionary at the time.

The combination of sampled attacks and synthesized sustain was actually pioneered by the Roland D-50, introduced in 1987 and one of the M1's main competitors back then. The main reason for this dual approach was to conserve onboard RAM, which was still very expensive. This sound generation method was then used by many other digital keyboards through the 1990s, until it became economically viable to store longer samples in the keyboard's onboard RAM.

The M1 also had a Combi mode enabling up to eight different sounds (programs) to play simultaneously, up to the unit's polyphony limitations. This structural hierarchy has been used and developed on all subsequent generations of Korg workstation keyboards. The unit featured an eight-track sequencer with up to 7,700 note capacity, with editing and quantization facilities. I used the M1 sequencer in my arranging classes at the Grove School of Music in Los Angeles, to play back various music examples to my students. Again, while decidedly basic by current standards, the M1's sequencer was a big deal at the time!

Perhaps the most famous sound from the M1 was its acoustic piano. This was very compressed, and not at all realistic-sounding by today's standards. However, it became a classic in its own right, and was used on many recordings. Here's an example in a "half-time" rock style, using the classic M1 piano sound:

TRACK 45

Half-time Rock

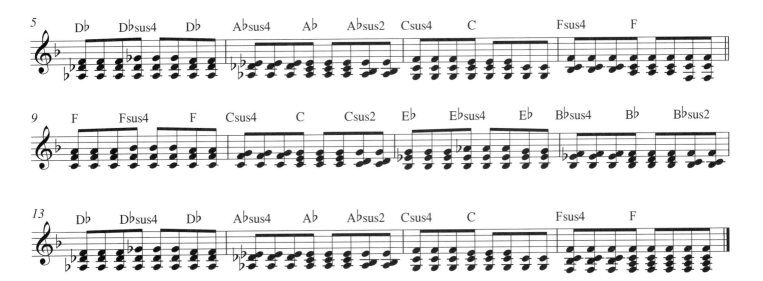

Listen to the track and you'll hear that the M1 piano is on the right channel, and the rest of the band is on the left channel. This piano was recorded using the Korg N364 keyboard (one of the successor generations of Korg workstations, introduced in 1996), which has the M1 piano as a "legacy sound" on the unit. The backing band on the left channel includes the "Fingered Bass" sample from the EXS24 software sampler within Logic and, from measure 9 onward, an electric guitar courtesy of the great RealStrat plug-in from MusicLab.

Harmony/Theory Notes

Note that this piano part consists of eighth-note chords throughout, using interior movements or resolutions (for example, the B♭ to A in measure 1, the F to E in measure 2, and so on). The half-time description refers to the drum groove, with the snare drum landing only on beat 4 of each measure, instead of the more typical 2 and 4. To put on my arranger's hat for a moment: Strictly speaking, the term half-time more correctly refers to the snare drum landing on beat 3; however, the term is also (more informally!) used to describe this particular type of situation.

MIDI

MIDI stands for **musical instrument digital interface**, and is a protocol that keyboards, computers, and other pieces of equipment use to communicate with each other. You can think of MIDI data as a "digital piano roll," containing information regarding which notes are played, their duration, volume, and so on. When MIDI technology first appeared back in the 1980s, there was great excitement at being able to play one keyboard and hear the sounds from another, having connected them with a MIDI cable. This is all very routine today, of course, but back then it was pretty revolutionary.

MIDI technology has several uses. Here are some of the more common ones if you are a performing musician and/or recording music in a home studio environment:

1. Connecting the "MIDI Out" from a controller keyboard (see p. 22) to the "MIDI In" of another sound source: either another MIDI keyboard as described above, or a MIDI rack module (a synthesizer and/or sample playback device without a physical keyboard attached), or a MIDI rack computer device (such as the Muse Receptor) that enables you to play back softsynths and plug-ins. You play the controller keyboard and hear the sound(s) of the

attached keyboard or module. If your controller keyboard also has onboard sounds, you can then layer and blend the sounds between the different sources.

2. Connecting the "MIDI Out" from a controller keyboard to the "MIDI In" of a MIDI interface connected to a Mac or PC (or, in some cases, directly to the computer). This will then enable you to get MIDI data into and out of your computer, which is useful in various ways including the following:

   a. If you are recording with digital audio workstation (DAW) software (see p. 26), the MIDI data recorded from your controller can then be used to trigger softsynths installed in your computer, and/or external MIDI devices in your system. The MIDI data can be edited and manipulated as needed in your DAW, and this process can then be repeated for each track/instrument in your song.

   b. If you are creating a chart or score with music notation software such as Finale or Sibelius, the MIDI data can be read by the software to produce the score. You'll still probably need to edit and further refine the score somewhat, but this is still much faster than creating the score from scratch. Most DAWs also have notation printing capabilities that are getting better all the time. However, for professional "publishing quality" notation I still prefer to use dedicated music notation software.

   c. If you have acquired MIDI files that you wish to play back and you don't want to use a standard MIDI file player program or your softsynths, you can route the MIDI data to any external MIDI device in your setup, to hear the MIDI files play back on that particular device.

MINIMOOG

The **Minimoog**, manufactured by Moog Music, is perhaps the most famous and revered analog synthesizer of all time. It was a monophonic (one note at a time) synthesizer, first released in 1970. Up to that point, analog synths were large, modular machines (see p. 76), so the groundbreaking all-in-one design of the Minimoog was largely responsible for synthesizers moving out of the studio and into the world of live performance.

The Minimoog has three voltage-controlled oscillators (VCOs), which then pass through a voltage-controlled filter (VCF) and a voltage-controlled amplifier (VCA). The units have separate envelopes (see p. 41) assigned to the filter and amplifier stages, which are actually referred to as ADSD envelopes (instead of the more typical ADSR), because both the decay and release times are controlled by a single knob. Technically, that might be considered something of a limitation, though it doesn't seem to concern the many users of this classic synth.

The Minimoog's filters use "transistor ladder" technology, a design patented by Moog Music. The Moog filter design is credited with imparting a uniquely warm, vibrant quality to the sound. In the 1970s the Minimoog was popularized by the progressive rock keyboardists Keith Emerson and Rick Wakeman. Emerson is credited with first developing pitch-bending techniques on the instrument, while Wakeman is famously quoted as saying that, with a Mini-moog, he could "for the first time, go out onstage and give the guitarist a run for his money."

Now we'll look at a couple of music examples using Minimoog-type sounds. Our first is in a progressive rock style, featuring a lead synth sound with a little glide (portamento, see p. 48) added:

TRACK 46

Progressive Rock

Listen to the track and you'll hear that the synth lead is on the right channel, and the rest of the band is on the left channel. The lead synth sound is a Minimoog emulation from the ES2 softsynth within Logic. The backing band on the left channel includes a bass sound from the EXS24 software sampler (again within Logic), and an organ preset (called "Wakeman") from the B4 virtual organ instrument (by Native Instruments).

Harmony/Theory Notes

Note that the synth solo part is arpeggiating the upper triads and/or extensions of the chords, using a 16th-note rhythmic subdivision. The drum groove is also placing the snare drum on beat 3 (instead of beat 4) in the odd-numbered measures (i.e., measures 1, 3, 5, etc.). All of this is typical of 1970s progressive rock—the band Yes, in particular.

Our next example is in a funk shuffle style, this time featuring a Minimoog-style bass synth sound:

TRACK 47

Listen to the track and you'll hear that the bass synth is on the right channel, with the rest of the band on the left channel. This example uses a swing-16ths feel. This time the Minimoog-style bass is from the Atmosphere softsynth (see p. 14). On the left channel, the backing band includes a nice "modeled" electric piano, courtesy of the EVP88 softsynth within Logic.

MODULAR SYNTHESIZER

A **modular synthesizer** consists of separate physical modules connected by patch cords. Early analog synthesizers in the 1960s were modular synthesizers, and these were followed by the all-in-one or integrated synthesizers such as the Minimoog (see p. 74) that were introduced in the 1970s. Here is a typical Moog modular system from the late 1960s:

Although there are many types of modules found on modular synthesizers, the following will be included in almost all systems:

- *Voltage-controlled oscillator (VCO)*: outputs a sound using a specific waveform (see p. 138). Common waveforms are sine (see p. 118), sawtooth (see p. 115), square (see p. 122), pulse (see p. 102), and triangle (see p. 132). Also see oscillator (p. 86).

- *Voltage-controlled filter (VCF)*: attenuates (reduces) frequencies depending upon the filter type and settings. See filter (p. 44).

- *Voltage-controlled amplifier (VCA)*: controls the amplitude (loudness). See amplifier (p. 9).

- *Envelope generator*: produces a voltage to create a one-time modification of another sound component, such as pitch, timbre, or volume. See envelope (p. 41).

- *Low-frequency oscillator (LFO)*: a low frequency waveform below the audio range, used to create a continuous, cyclical modification of another sound component, such as pitch, timbre, or loudness. See LFO (p. 71).

By the mid-1970s, modular synths had fallen out of favor, as more musicians were using the portable all-in-one keyboard synthesizers of the time. At the present time, however, modular synths are making something of a comeback in the softsynth world. Software synths/plug-ins such as Native Instruments' Reaktor (see p. 105) and Applied Acoustics Systems Tassman offer a whole world of modular synth flexibility, limited only by the power of your computer. Also, the software company Arturia has created highly authentic softsynth emulations of classic modular synths, such as the Moog Modular and the (semi-modular) ARP 2600.

MODULATION

In the synthesizer world, **modulation** is the process of continuously varying a component of the sound, creating a particular effect or sonic characteristic. Some of the more commonly used types of modulation are listed as follows:

- *Amplitude Modulation* occurs when the amplifier stage is modulated, for example, by a low-frequency oscillator (LFO, p. 71) to produce a tremolo effect (see p. 131). [Note that we are not talking here about amplitude modulation (or AM) as the term applies to radio waves or communication technology.]

- *Filter Modulation* occurs when the filter stage is modulated, for example, by an LFO to produce a wah-wah or filter-sweep effect.

- *Frequency Modulation* (see p. 45) is a synthesis method that modulates a simple waveform with another waveform in the audio range, creating complex sounds.

- *Pitch Modulation* occurs when the pitch of a sound is modulated, for example, by a low-frequency oscillator (LFO, see p. 71) to produce a vibrato effect (see p. 136).

- *Ring Modulation* is the product of taking two different waveforms and then outputting the sum and difference of the frequencies present in each waveform. This resulting signal is rich in overtones, and useful for metallic and bell-like sounds. This feature was commonly implemented on early modular synthesizers (see p. 76), but was less common on all-in-one analog synthesizers and workstation keyboards. However, with the advent of physical modeling (see p. 89) and softsynths, ring modulation has had something of a resurgence in popularity.

MODULATION WHEEL

On a synthesizer, the **modulation wheel** (or **mod wheel**) is a controller in the shape of a wheel, normally to the immediate left of the lowest note on the keyboard. The wheel is imbedded in the surface of the unit, so that only the top part is visible. Movement of the wheel is then used to add expression or to modulate some aspect of the sound. This is normally a programmable function, meaning that the mod wheel's effect can be programmed within a particular sound (or program) on the synthesizer. Typical uses of the mod wheel include the following:

- adding vibrato (repetitive variation in pitch, see p. 136).

- changing the timbre of the sound by altering the filter cut-off frequency (see p. 44).

- adding or altering effects (see p. 39): for example, increasing the reverb, or changing the speed of rotary speaker emulation.

- detuning (or increasing the "out-of-tuneness") between two oscillators.

The following example contains two single notes, and demonstrates two of these mod wheel usages: the timbre change (on the first note), and the detuning between two oscillators (on the second note). The simple analog synth sound used is from the ES2 softsynth within Logic.

TRACK 48

First note:
For this synth program, the mod wheel is routed to the filter cutoff point. The note starts off fairly dark, due to the filter's low cutoff frequency. Then as the mod wheel is moved, the note gets brighter as the cutoff is raised, which then "opens" the filter.

Second note:
For this synth program, the mod wheel is routed to the detuning between the oscillators. The note starts off "in tune." Then as the mod wheel is moved, the note gets progressively more "out-of-tune" as the oscillators are slightly detuned from one another. Then as the mod wheel is moved back, the note becomes "in tune" again.

MONOPHONIC SYNTHESIZER

A **monophonic synthesizer** has the ability to sound only one note at a time. The first analog synthesizers were almost always monophonic, although some early units, notably the ARP Odyssey and the Moog Sonic Six, offered duophonic (two-note) capability. By the late 1970s, polyphonic synthesizers (with the ability to sound multiple notes at once) began to emerge. See p. 95 for more information on polyphonic synthesizers.

Although the arrival of polyphonic synthesizers was very significant, this did not mean that monophonic synthersizers were no longer used. For example, musicians playing synth bass or lead parts (two of the most common uses for classic analog synths) need only one note at a time. So, monophonic and polyphonic synths are often found side-by-side in today's professional keyboard rigs.

It is desirable for modern keyboard synthesizers (and softsynths) to be able to emulate a monophonic playing mode (mono mode) to prevent multiple notes from "overlapping." Some synthesizers offer a *legato* option within the monophonic mode, which prevents the note from being "re-triggered" as long as a key is being held down on the keyboard. We'll now demonstrate these playing options with the following music example:

TRACK 49

Note that this example contains multiple parts on the same staff. For example, in measure 1 the first A (whole note) lasts for four beats, and this is held while the remaining notes are played during the measure.

This track uses an analog lead synth sound from the ES2 softsynth within Logic, and is played three times with exactly the same playing technique each time: the low A is played and held down by the thumb at the beginning of each measure, while the other notes are played with the upper fingers of the right hand. However, the sound is very different each time, depending on the playing mode setting on the synthesizer:

Poly (polyphonic) mode	For the initial performance of this example, the synth is in **poly mode**. This is the normal (default) mode for most synths. Each part in the example is played, and all notes "trigger" their respective envelopes, which for this sound results in a short, pronounced attack for each note.
Mono (monophonic) mode	The second time, the synth is in **mono mode**. This allows only one note to be played at one time (which is always the most recent note played on the keyboard, if more than one note is being held down). So in this music example, the low A "cuts out" when the high A is played, halfway through beat 1. Then at the start of beat 2, the low A is "re-triggered" when the high A is released on the keyboard. This is again "cut out" by the G that follows, and so on.
Legato mode	The third time, the synth is in **legato mode**. This is a type of mono mode where the envelopes are not re-triggered as long as a note is being held down on the keyboard. As soon as all notes are released, the very next note will re-trigger, and so on. In this example, we hear only the short attack of the first A in each measure; the other notes sound smooth and legato, as their envelopes are not re-triggering. Then because all the notes are released right before the second measure, the envelopes are re-triggered for the first A in that measure, and so on.

MOOG

R.A. Moog Co. was founded by Robert Moog in 1953. His company became Moog Music in 1972. Moog's name became synonymous with synthesizers, and he developed synthesizer components such as voltage-controlled oscillators (see p. 86) and envelope generators (see p. 41) that have since become standard. Moog created the first subtractive synthesizer (see p. 122) to be controlled by a keyboard, which he debuted at the annual Audio Engineering Society (AES) trade show in 1964. His first instruments were modular synthesizers (see

p. 76), which were shipped with a piano-style keyboard, unlike the other synthesizers of the time. By the early 1970s, Moog Music switched to making portable, all-in-one synthesizers, including the Minimoog (see p. 74), perhaps the most famous synth of all time.

In 1975, Moog released the Taurus bass pedal synthesizer, which was similar in design to organ pedals, but used to control or "trigger" synthesized bass sounds. The Taurus produced a very fat and characteristic analog bass sound, and was used by many top artists including Parliament-Funkadelic, Pink Floyd, Yes, and the Electric Light Orchestra. Also around this time the Polymoog was introduced, as part of the first wave of polyphonic synthesizers available. Although superceded by later products such as Sequential Circuits' Prophet-5 (see p. 99) and Yamaha's CS-80, the Polymoog was groundbreaking at the time, and was adopted as a signature sound by the 1980s synth-pop artist Gary Numan. Other prominent Polymoog users included Rick Wakeman (Yes) and Tony Banks (Genesis).

Moog Music went through various changes of ownership in the 1970s, culminating in being sold to Norlin (the owners of Gibson guitars). Robert Moog then left his own company in 1977, and for many years was unable to produce synthesizers under his own name. Moog Music continued to produce synthesizers in the 1980s, notably the Moog Source and the Memorymoog. Finally, in 2001 Robert Moog's company, Big Briar Music, was able to reacquire the name Moog Music, and in 2002 released the acclaimed Minimoog Voyager. This is a 21st-century re-creation of the classic Minimoog, with modern-day features such as patch storage, MIDI control and a pressure-sensitive keyboard.

With the release of the Little Phatty monophonic synthesizer in 2006, Moog Music is still going strong. Like the Voyager, the Little Phatty combines classic analog sound with up-to-date features, but at a more affordable price.

MOTIF

The **Yamaha Motif** is one of the most popular workstation-style keyboards in the late 2000s, alongside similarly-priced competitors such as Roland's Fantom (see p. 44) and Korg's M3 series. These machines have a great selection of onboard sounds, multiple effects (see p. 39), and multitrack sequencing/recording capability. The Motif series currently consists of the flagship XS8 model (88 weighted keys) and the smaller XS7 (76 unweighted keys) and XS6 (61 unweighted keys) models.

The Motif series offers an integrated sampling sequencer, with studio-style mixing functions and effects. The latest Motif XS workstations have an expanded sequencer capability of 130,000 notes, and also include new strings, drums, and acoustic piano sounds. The acoustic piano is reasonably good, and better than in earlier Motif versions, but not quite as good as some other "stage pianos" or software instruments. The unit includes eight knobs and eight sliders to control various parameters, and over 350MB of waveforms in ROM (read-only memory), which is fairly good by today's standards. Although the onboard sounds in earlier Motifs could be supplemented via Yamaha's PLG expansion boards, this feature is not implemented in the current Motif XS series, which can pose a problem for users wishing to upgrade to a newer Motif.

An honorable mention should also go to Yamaha's S90 series of performance keyboards, which basically have the Motif sounds "under the hood," but do not have the sampling, sequencing, and mixing features of the Motif. Many musicians will not need these features in a keyboard, if they use a computer-based digital audio workstation (DAW, see p. 26) to produce music. I have used an S90 on many gigs with a Steely Dan tribute band and, like the Motif, it has good all-round sonic capability, notably including some excellent electric piano sounds. I have also seen S90s and Motifs being used by many other keyboardists over the years, and these machines are a worthy addition to any player's rig.

MULTI-TIMBRAL

A **multi-timbral synthesizer** is capable of sounding more than one instrument or timbre simultaneously. Don't confuse this with "polyphonic," which is the ability to sound more than one note at once. Polyphonic synthesizers (see p. 95) need not be multi-timbral, although many are, particularly these days. Synthesizers, samplers (see p. 112), and workstation keyboards (see p. 140) can all be multi-timbral.

Here are some common uses for multi-timbral instruments:

- *Live performance splits*, assigning one sound (say, an acoustic bass) to the left of a split point on the keyboard, and another sound (say, a piano) to the right of the split point. This enables the player to play both the bass and piano part, one in each hand.

- *Live performance layers*, assigning two or more sounds to the keyboard or to a region of the keyboard. For example, you might layer a synth or string pad sound on top of a piano sound. I do this regularly on gigs with my Kurzweil PC3 keyboard, with the pad layer being controlled by a volume pedal.

- *Onboard sequencing* (using the sequencer within a workstation synth). When using the sequencer in a modern workstation synth such as the Yamaha Motif or the Roland Fantom, the unit will need to respond multi-timbrally—i.e., be able to play back instruments such as piano, bass, drums, etc. simultaneously.

- *External sequencing* (using the synthesizer as a MIDI sound module). This could be done in a computer-based digital audio workstation (DAW) setup, or by a hardware sequencer. If the DAW is sending out MIDI data for more than one instrument (using different MIDI channels) to the synthesizer, it will again need to respond multi-timbrally to play back multiple instruments.

Don't forget that a synthesizer's multi-timbral capability is ultimately limited by its total polyphony (number of "voices" that can sound at any one time). To take a simple example: if your synth had only eight-voice polyphony, and you use up four notes for a piano part (each of which uses one voice), you have only four voices left for a guitar part. If at any one time your piano and guitar part together use more than eight voices in total, then "note-stealing" occurs (the oldest notes are cut off). Some synths allow you to prioritize the allocation of voices to certain instruments, in case you run into this problem.

NOISE GENERATOR

In a synthesizer, a **noise generator** is an oscillator that produces noise instead of a pitched waveform. Noise is an important component of many synthesized sounds, including "breathy" synth pads, seashore and wind sound effects, and electronic percussion sounds, to name just a few.

Different types of noise have different combinations of frequencies, and are described with colors (white noise, pink noise, etc.). This is an analogy to the appearance of colors with a similar frequency makeup. For example, white noise has all frequencies equally represented, and is called "white" because white light contains all optical frequencies. White noise has a very bright sound, and is used to synthesize electronic drum sounds such as snare drums, hi-hats, and crash cymbals.

Pink noise is also commonly used, and sounds darker than white noise. In pink noise, every octave (successive doubling of the frequency) contains the same energy and volume, which is why this type of noise is used as a reference signal by engineers. Pink noise can be derived by applying a low-pass filter (see p. 44) to white noise, progressively attenuating the higher frquencies. Pink noise is very useful as a component in warm-sounding synth pads, and in generating ocean wave effects.

Here are examples of white noise and pink noise, produced using the Atmosphere softsynth (see p. 14):

TRACK 50

The first noise segment on this track is a *white noise* example.

The second noise segment on this track is a *pink noise* example.

Here are some more noise types you may encounter:

- *Red noise* is darker than pink noise, with more filtering of the upper frequencies (a "steeper slope" applied to the low-pass filter).

- *Blue noise* is equivalent to white noise passed through a high-pass filter, leaving minimal low frequencies and a lot of high frequencies.

- *Grey noise* boosts the lowest and highest frequencies, giving a perception of being equally loud at all frequencies, due to the natural bias of the human ear.

Many classic synthesizers (including the Minimoog, see p. 74) include a noise generator as one of their sound sources. This trend continues in the 21st century, in softsynths such as Logic's ES2 and Native Instruments' Reaktor (see p. 105).

OASYS

The **Korg Oasys** is the ultimate high-end workstation synthesizer, released in 2005. It has an "open architecture" system that is expandable via software updates. The Oasys hardware has components found in most personal computers, including a Pentium CPU, a hard disk drive, and user-expandable RAM, as well as a very striking 10.4 inch LCD touch screen. The word OASYS is an acronym for Korg's Open Architecture SYnthesis Studio, which enables several synthesizer engines to run simultaneously. The Oasys series currently consists of the flagship Oasys88 model (88 weighted keys) and the smaller Oasys76 model (76 unweighted keys).

The current Oasys keyboards include the following onboard synthesis engines:

- HD-1, a combined sample-playback (see p. 112) and wavetable (see p. 139) synthesizer

- AL-1, a virtual analog synthesizer (emulates traditional analog synthesis using digital signal processing)

- CX-3, a modeled tone-wheel organ instrument (based on Korg's popular CX-3 electric organ)

- STR-1, a physical modeling synth (see p. 89) for plucked string instruments

- MOD-7, a semi-modular synth combining several synthesis methods, including sample playback and subtractive synthesis (see p. 122)

- LAC-1 (Optional bundle), including emulations of two classic Korg synths: the Polysix and the MS20.

The Oasys excels in the normal areas covered by workstation synthesizers. It has an integrated 16-track sequencer with powerful features and is easy to use, thanks to the large LCD touch screen. Unlike most workstation sequencers, the Oasys sequencer has power and flexibility comparable to many computer-based DAW setups. It can also mix tracks with studio-quality effects and burn an audio CD. It also has good audio recording facilities (up to four audio tracks can be recorded at once), as well as state-of-the-art sampling (see p. 112) and sample editing capabilities. The Oasys also functions as a high-end controller keyboard (see p. 22), with eight velocity-sensitive drum pads, and an assortment of faders, knobs, joysticks, and butttons that can be programmed to control various instrument functions. In short, if you have the budget, this machine rocks!

For the majority of musicians whose budget doesn't quite stretch to an Oasys, it's good to know that Korg's Oasys technology is trickling down to some of their more affordable synthesizers, including their M3 series of workstations. Current versions of the M3 include Korg's Enhanced Definition Synthesis (EDS), which is based on the Oasys HD-1 synthesis engine. The M3 also includes the latest version of KARMA (Korg's system for generating complex musical phrases in realtime, developed by Stephen Kay) which was previously implemented in the Oasys.

OBERHEIM

Oberheim Electronics was founded by the engineer Tom Oberheim in 1973, and was a noted manufacturer of synthesizers and electronic musical instruments in the 1970s and 1980s. Oberheim is credited with inventing the first polyphonic synsthesizers in the mid-1970s, the Oberheim Two-Voice and Four-Voice. Multiple voice capability was achieved by hard-wiring multiple monophonic synthesizers together, each of which had to be independently programmed. These synths were revolutionary in their time, but were later superceded by the Sequential Circuits' Prophet-5 (see p. 99), which had five-note polyphony with a single set of sound-shaping controls, as well as patch memory capability.

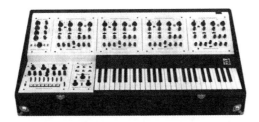

Not to be outdone, Oberheim brought out the more portable OB-X polyphonic synthesizer in 1979, in direct competition with the Prophet-5. The OB-X was available in four-, six-, and eight-voice configurations, and was fairly expensive (just the four-voice version was over $4,000!). However, the OB-X had a uniquely warm and "fat" sound, and was used by many top artists at the time, including Prince, Van Halen, Queen, Billy Joel, and Bruce Hornsby. The OB-X was followed by various other Oberheim synths, notably including the Matrix series (Matrix 6 and Matrix 12, offering 6- and 12-voice polyphony respectively). In particular, the Matrix 12 had very deep programming capabilities, and was known for its very thick analog pads, basses, filter sweeps, and more. The characteristic sound of the Matrix 12 was used on recordings by Vangelis, Depeche Mode, Technotronic, and many others.

Oberheim Electronics was acquired by the Gibson Guitar Corporation in 1986, who later licensed the Oberheim name to Viscount, an Italian organ manufacturer. Viscount then manufactured several electronic instruments, including the Oberheim OB12 digital polyphonic synthesizer introduced in 2002.

In addition to their classic range of synthesizers, it should be noted that Oberheim produced one of the most important drum machines ever—the DMX, which debuted in 1981. This was the main competitor to the Linn LM-1 drum machine at the time, and helped to reshape the popular music of the 1980s. The DMX was used on many landmark recordings of the period, including Herbie Hancock's "Rockit" and Madonna's "Holiday." The DMX's sound was also very influential in the development of early hip hop styles, and the rapper Earl Simmons (known as DMX) took his name from this legendary drum machine.

OSCILLATOR

In the synthesizer world, the **oscillator** is the component that outputs the initial waveform for the sound. In basic analog synthesis (see p. 10), the oscillator stage is the first of the three main sound components, followed by the filter (see p. 44) and amplifier (see p. 9). The components in early synthesizers were voltage-controlled, so the oscillator stage was referred to as a "voltage controlled oscillator" (VCO) in classic analog synthesizers. However, with the advent of digital synthesis (see p. 29), these synthesizer functions were re-created digitally, and the term "digitally controlled oscillator" (DCO) was then used by some synth manufacturers.

Since the 1970s, most synthesizers have featured at least two oscillators, which can be blended together and passed through the filter and amplifier sections. The oscillators in earlier analog synthesizers produced basic waveforms (such as sawtooth, sine, square, or triangle; see entries for these waveforms). In modern-day synthesizers, the oscillator stage might produce more complex waveforms, as well as samples (digital recording of another instrument or sound; see p. 112). The pitch of the oscillator(s) in a synthesizer can be controlled by the low-frequency oscillator (LFO, see p. 71) to create a vibrato effect (see p. 136).

The Korg M1 (see p. 72) was a notable example of a workstation synthesizer that could blend samples with more traditional synthesized waveforms. For example, in an M1 sound program you could set Oscillator 1 to a Piano sample, and Oscillator 2 to an analog synth sound (for example, using a sawtooth waveform). These could be blended together, passed through a common filter and envelopes, and so on. This is somewhat routine these days, but in the late 1980s, when the M1 was introduced, it was a big deal.

Synthesizer oscillators may also be modulated in other ways. For example, a square wave (see p. 122) can have its pulse width modulated (typically by the low-frequency oscillator or LFO) to give a detuning-type effect. Also, in the frequency modulation or FM method of synthesis (see p. 45), the output of one oscillator (in the audio range) is used to modulate the frequency of another oscillator, creating complex sounds rich in harmonic content.

PAD

The term **pad** or **synth pad** is used in two different ways—as a music arrangement term and as a sound description:

- In a music arrangement context, a synth pad is a sustained musical part played on a synthesizer. Normally a synth pad will use two or more notes at once, although the term is sometimes used to refer to single-note sustained lines.

- In a sound description context, a synth pad is a sustained, mellow sound suitable for background harmony and texture. Pad sounds often have slow attacks (see p. 17) and have string- or vocal-like characteristics that help them "blend in" with the track. Many of today's keyboard synthesizers and softsynths have one or more preset banks of pads.

Some synthesizers are particularly noted for the quality of their pads. In concerts performed by the Grammy-winning contemporary jazz group Yellowjackets, keyboardist Russ Ferrante still uses the characteristic warm, analog pads from his Korg 01/W (an older generation of Korg's workstation synthesizers). In the softsynth world, the main reason that Atmosphere (see p. 14) has been so successful is the quality and depth of its pad sounds, even though it also includes a great selection of other types of sounds.

Now we'll check out a music example in a neo-soul style, which uses a synth pad in its arrangement:

TRACK 51

Neo-Soul

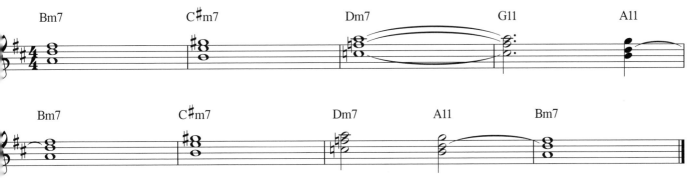

Listen to the track and you'll hear that the synth pad is on the right channel, with the rest of the band on the left channel. Try listening to the track both with and without the pad (i.e., by turning down the right channel), and you can also experiment with the level of the pad that you think is appropriate. Most mixing engineers I know prefer not to mix the synth pads at too high a level—the pads are a subtle glue that can hold the track together, and would be missed if they weren't there.

The pad in this case is produced from Native Instruments' Massive softsynth, using a blend of sawtooth and square waveforms, plus some noise to add breathiness to the sound. The backing band includes a Moog-style synth bass from the Atmosphere softsynth, and a "modeled" Rhodes electric piano from the EVP88 softsynth within Logic.

Harmony/Theory Notes

The above synth pad part makes use of upper structure triads. For example, the right hand notes on the Bm7 chord form a D major triad (D F♯ A). These are the 3rd, 5th, and 7th of the Bm7 chord, and can be thought of as a major triad (D major in this case) built from the 3rd of the chord (Bm7 in this case). Other upper structure triads are also used in this example, as follows:

- the right hand notes on the C♯m7 chord form an E major triad (built from the 3rd of the chord)

- the right hand notes on the Dm7 chord form an F major triad (built from the 3rd of the chord)

- the right hand notes on the G11 chord form an F major triad (built from the 7th of the chord)

- the right hand notes on the A11 chord form a G major triad (built from the 7th of the chord)

PATCH

In the synthesizer world, a **patch** is a sound setting that can be stored in the memory of the unit and then recalled for live performance purposes. For example, on your synth you are likely to have patches for brass sounds, for string sounds, and so on. The first widely available polyphonic synth to offer patch storage and recall was the Sequential Circuits' Prophet-5 (see p. 99).

The term "patch" originated from the days of modular synthesizers (see p. 76) in the 1960s. These machines had separate physical modules that were connected by patch cords. Modular synthesizers had no memory in which to save the various parameters, so musicians at the time wrote down the knob positions and the location of the patch cables on a piece of paper known as a "patch sheet." Ever since, "patch" has been used to describe an overall sound setting, even though most players don't use patch cords and patch sheets anymore.

The term "patch" is also used interchangeably with "program." For example, on workstation synths such as Korg's N364 and Kurzweil's PC3, a program is a basic sound setting (including oscillators/waveforms, filters, and so on) that can be recalled, edited, and saved in the unit's memory. By contrast, on Yamaha's popular S90 performance keyboard, this basic sound setting is referred to as a "voice" (which may be confusing, since this term is commonly used in the context of a synthesizer's polyphony, i.e., how many "voices" the unit can sound simultaneously).

Most modern-era workstation synthesizers also have a "hierarchical level" above the patch or program level in which combinations of programs can be stored (e.g., for performace splits or layers, or for multi-timbral use; see p. 81). This hierarchical level has various names, depending on the manufacturer. For example, Korg calls it a Combination, Yamaha calls it a Performance, and Kurzweil calls it a Setup. So be prepared for some inconsistent terminology between the different manufacturers.

Today's synthesizers can import and export patch and other information via MIDI System Exclusive (SysEx) commands. This is typically done to back up the program data on a computer, or to use computer-based patch editing software, which often is easier and more flexible than editing a patch directly on the unit itself.

PHASE DISTORTION

Phase distortion is a synthesis method developed by Casio in the mid-1980s, and implemented in their CZ series of synthesizers. This technology has similarities to frequency modulation (FM synthesis, see p. 45). Phase distortion works by modifying the phase angle of basic sine waves to produce a wide variety of other waveforms, and to simulate filter sweeps and resonance. Casio's CZ-101 was their first synthesizer to use this technology, and was derided by some players at the time due to its miniature keys (instead of full-sized keys) and 49-note keyboard (instead of the normal minimum of 61 keys). However, it was still a price/performance breakthrough upon its introduction in 1984, as it was the first fully programmable polyphonic synth for under $500.

For musicians in the mid-1980s who wanted to jump on the digital synth bandwagon, but whose budget didn't quite stretch to the Yamaha DX7 (see p. 36), the Casio CZ series of synths was an affordable alternative. Not to be outdone, Yamaha then released their own lower-cost digital synths (including the DX21 and DX100) to compete with the Casio synths.

Like the Yamaha DX series, the Casio synths were thought of as having a "thinner" sound than the analog synths of the period, but with the capability of producing bright and edgy "digital" sounds. The CZ series also had sophisticated eight-stage envelope generators (see p. 41), allowing for very flexible sound shaping and editing.

By the 1990s, phase distortion had largely been superceded by other synthesis methods and technologies. However, in the 21st century, phase distortion synthesis lives on, thanks to Musicrow's White Crow softsynth, which faithfully re-creates the Casio CZ series sounds, but with modern-day features and effects added.

PHYSICAL MODELING

Physical modeling is a synthesis technology that uses algorithms and equations to digitally duplicate the physical characteristics of a particular instrument. Parameter values are entered that affect the "modeled" sound. For example, in a modeled violin instrument, values might be entered to describe the width of the bow, the resonance of the strings, the soundboard response, and so on. Similarly, in a modeled guitar instrument you might see parameters for string thickness, pick characteristics (how hard or soft), distance from the bridge where the string is plucked, and so on. Modeling can also create unique instruments, by using parameter values that have no real-world equivalent: for example, a piano with a 30-foot soundboard, or a guitar with strings one inch thick.

Physical modeling is often compared to sampling (see p. 112), as both synthesis methods are used to emulate the sound of an existing instrument. As you might expect, both approaches have their pros and cons. When you play a note using a trumpet sound on a sample-playback synth, what you hear is an exact digital recording of the trumpet. However, it is often difficult to impart expressiveness to a musical phrase (like a real trumpet player would) when you're simply playing back samples. By contrast, when playing a trumpet sound using a modeling instrument, you might be able to vary parameters such as lip tension, blowing pressure, valve positions, and so on. All this should lead to a more expressive and authentic performance. How realistic it actually sounds will depend in part on how good the modeled instrument or softsynth is. Not surprisingly, this will be a matter of opinion (and debate!) among musicians.

Another important difference between physical modeling and sampling is in the processing power and storage/memory that is needed. Sample playback needs less processing power, but more memory and/or disk drive capacity. Conversely, physical modeling can be very processor-intensive, but doesn't need the storage capacity since samples are not being used.

Physical modeling became possible on keyboard synthesizers due to the increase in digital signal processing (DSP) power that was available by the 1990s. The first commercially available synthesizer to use modeling technology was the Yamaha VL1, released in 1994. At the time, it was considered a bold move for Yamaha to release a monophonic synthesizer, as virtually all other synths were polyphonic instruments. However, the expressiveness and realism of the VL1 was groundbreaking: for example, you could dial up a brass sound and then change the lip pressure just by moving the modulation wheel.

Other notable keyboard synthesizers using physical modeling were Korg's Prophecy and Z1 synths. The Prophecy (introduced in 1995) was a monophonic synth with a 37-note keyboard, and the Z1 (introduced in 1997) was a polyphonic synth with a 61-note keyboard. These synths have been used by top artists such as Yes, Radiohead, Orbital, and BT.

In the 21st century, increasingly sophisticated softsynths using physical modeling are posssible, due to the increase in computer power now available. An interesting example is Modartt's Pianoteq, a modeled virtual piano instrument. I had a chance to play and compare this piano to the sample-based Ivory (see p. 56). The Pianoteq piano had a very clean sound, with good velocity response and many adjustable parameters including the tuning. However, I think Ivory still had the edge in terms of warmth and realism. Again, this is a matter of opinion, and reasonable minds may differ.

Now we'll look at a couple of physical modeling synthesis examples using Sculpture, a modeled synth plug-in included with Logic. The first example is in an instrumental New Age style and features a solo acoustic guitar playing arpeggio patterns. Note that this is not a sample of an acoustic guitar; the sound has been synthesized using the physical modeling capabilities within Sculpture.

TRACK 52

New Age

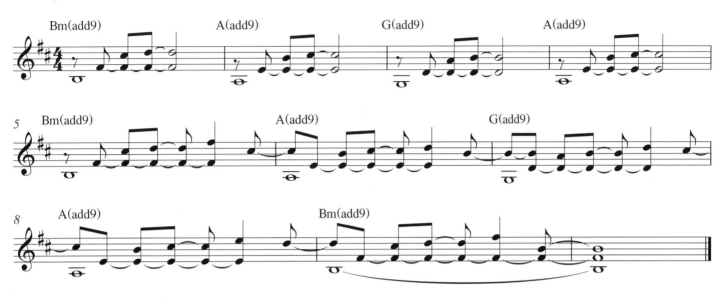

Harmony/Theory Notes

This part sounds an octave lower than actually written, for consistency with normal (or non-synthesized) guitar writing. The guitar is a transposing instrument, and a guitarist will play one octave lower than written on the guitar part.

Our next example is in a pop/funk style, featuring a modeled marimba sound from Sculpture:

TRACK 53

Pop/Funk

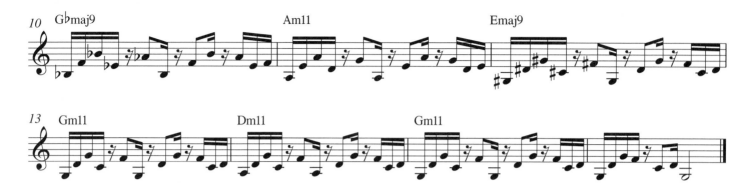

Listen to the track and you'll hear the modeled marimba sound on the right channel, and the rest of the band (including the Scarbee slap bass and a chorused Rhodes piano from Applied Acoustic Systems' Lounge Lizard) on the left channel.

Harmony/Theory Notes

This marimba part is derived from minor pentatonic scales. In the first two measures, the line over the Am11 chord is derived from the A minor pentatonic scale (A C D E G). Similarly, in the next two measures, the line over the Gm11 chord is derived from the G minor pentatonic scale (G B♭ C D F). These lines are then repeated over the following Fmaj9 and E♭maj9 chords, and so on. Also, no key signature has been written, as the keys are changing frequently in this example.

Other notable softsynths using physical modeling are Applied Acoustics Systems' String Studio (for guitars, basses, harps, and bowed instruments), and Arturia's Brass (for trumpets, trombones, and saxophones).

PITCH BEND

On a synthesizer, **pitch bend** occurs as a result of moving the **pitch bend wheel**, which is normally located to the left of the lowest note on the keyboard. When the wheel is moved up from its center postion, the pitch is sharped; when the wheel is moved down from its center postion, the pitch is flatted. The amount of pitch bend (i.e., the degree to which the pitch is sharped or flatted) is a programmable function on modern-day synthesizers.

Most sound programs (or patches, see p. 88) have a default pitch bend setting of a whole step. If you play the note C on a synth with this pitch bend setting, and then move the wheel all the way up, the pitch of the note will slide up to a D. If you want the pitch to bend up only by a half-step (to C♯), you have to use your ears to determine when the wheel has been moved far enough. This is an important skill for synth lead and bass players to acquire.

Although the whole-step bend range is the most common, this can be adjusted (for example, to the interval of a 5th or to an octave) depending on the player's style and preference. Most modern synths have a spring-loaded mechanism to return the pitch bend wheel to the center position, and a "deadband" right around this center position, in which no pitch change occurs. It wasn't always like this, though. Back when the Minimoog (see p. 74) was first introduced in 1970, its pitch bend wheel had no spring-loading and no "deadzone" in the center. This was actually preferred by some players, who used rapid movements of the wheel to impart a "real-time" vibrato and nuance to their performance.

Our first music example is in a funk shuffle style, and applies pitch bend techniques to a synth bass. Here the pitch bend setting is the normal default of a whole-step, so I'm using my ears to make sure the half-step bends are correct in the bass part:

TRACK 54

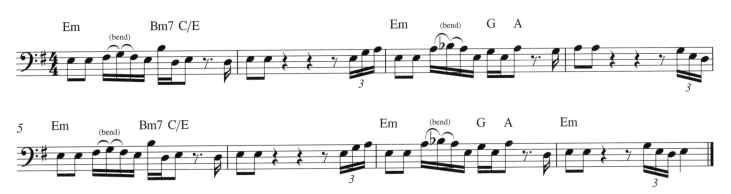

Listen to the track and you'll hear that the synth bass sound is on the right channel, and the rest of the band is on the left channel. Note that this example uses swing 16ths. Fire up a bass patch (with whole-step pitch bend) on your favorite synth and try playing along! Don't forget to listen to your pitch bends, to check that you are playing the half-step intervals correctly.

This Moog-style bass sound was produced by Applied Acoustic Systems' Ultra Analog modeling synth. On the left channel, the backing band includes an organ pad from the Native Instruments' B4 plug-in, a staccato comping synth from their FM8 softsynth, and acoustic drums courtesy of the BFD2 virtual drum instrument.

Harmony/Theory Notes

Like most funk bass lines, this one covers the roots of the chord at the "points of chord change," with some 16th-note rhythmic embellishments in between. The bass phrases can also be thought of in terms of scale sources. For example, the first two measures (including the F♯-G bend in measure 1) come from the E natural minor scale, and the next two measures (including the A-B♭ bend in measure 3) come from the E blues scale, hence the "bluesy" quality of the bass line in measure 3.

Our next example is in an R&B ballad style, and uses pitch bend on a lead synth sound. This time the part requires whole-step bends, so I'm moving the pitch bend wheel all the way up and back again. As before, the wheel has the default setting of a whole-step range.

TRACK 55

R&B Ballad

Listen to the track and you'll hear that the lead synth is on the right channel, with the rest of the band on the left channel. The lead synth is a "digital mono lead" from the FM8 soft-synth, designed to emulate the characteristics of an EWI (electronic wind instrument, a synth controller for woodwind players). On the left channel, the backing band includes a synth bass from the Atmosphere softsynth, and a synth pad from Native Instruments' Massive softsynth.

Harmony/Theory Notes

This synth part is created mostly from pentatonic scales, built from the root or 5th of the major chords, and from the 7th of the suspended dominant chords. For example, the figure in measure 1 is derived from the C pentatonic scale (C D E G A), built from the root of the Cmaj9 and the 5th of the Fmaj9 chords respectively. Similarly, the figure in measure 2 is derived from the F pentatonic scale (F G A C D), built from the 5th of the B♭maj9 and the 7th of the G11 chords respectively.

Further Reading

For more information on using pentatonic and blues scales over different chords, please check out my *Contemporary Music Theory*, *Level Two* book, published by Hal Leonard Corporation.

PLUG-IN

In the computer world, a **plug-in** is a computer program that interacts with a host application to perform a specific function. For 21st-century musicians, the term most commonly refers to a program working in tandem with a digital audio workstation (DAW, see p. 26). These days, computer music plug-ins normally fall into one of the following broad categories:

- *Softsynths* (also known as virtual instruments, see p. 119). Instruments such as Atmosphere (see p. 14), Ivory (see p. 56), and Kontakt (see p. 61) can "plug into" (and be accessible from) a DAW host. Softsynths may be emulations of acoustic instruments or classic synthesizers, or they can be "original" instruments with their own distinctive sound. Softsynths often come in stand-alone as well as plug-in versions (i.e., they can function with or without a host).

- *Effects* (see p. 39). Manufacturers such as McDSP, Line 6, and IK Multimedia produce effects plug-ins for reverb, distortion, echo, amplifier simulation ("amp-sims"), and so on. Currently, most DAW hosts also come with a suite of "internal" effects plug-ins, so it's a judgement call as to whether or not you need to supplement the effects in your DAW with third-party plug-ins.

- *Mixing and mastering*. Manufacturers such as Waves, Sonnox, and Eventide produce plug-ins used for mixing and mastering: compression, limiting, equalization, emulation of classic audio processors and mixing desks, and so on. (There is some overlap between this category and the effects category.)

- *Pitch correction*. For years, the Antares plug-in Auto-Tune was the industry standard for pitch correction, but more recently Celemony's Melodyne has emerged as a serious competitor, with the ability to handle polyphonic audio material.

- *Virtual instrument design*. Plug-ins such as Native Instruments' Reaktor (see p. 105), Applied Acoustic Systems' Tassman, and Cycling 74's Max/MSP enable you to design and build your own virtual synthesizers from the ground up. This process is not for the faint-hearted, but if you're willing to work at it, you can open up whole new worlds of sonic creativity.

Plug-ins conform to a "system-level format" such as Steinberg's VST (Virtual Studio Technology, see p. 137), Apple's AU (Audio Units), and Digidesign's RTAS (Real-Time Audio Suite) or TDM (Time-Division Multiplexing). The choice of plug-in format will depend on the DAW host you use and the computer you have. For example, Steinberg's Cubase uses VST format plug-ins, Apple's Logic and MOTU's Digital Performer use AU format plug-ins, Digidesign's ProTools uses RTAS or TDM format plug-ins, and so on. If you're buying a plug-in, check that it's available in the right format for your setup, and make sure you install the correct version. Most plug-in installation CDs or DVDs include versions for different formats.

The majority of instrument and effects plug-ins will work in multiple DAW hosts, subject to the above format issues. For example, MOTU's Symphonic Instrument plug-in works in all major DAW hosts, including MOTU's own Digital Performer (see p. 27). A major exception to this principle is Digidesign, who have created a range of instrument plug-ins that will work only in their ProTools (see p. 100) host DAW.

POLYPHONIC SYNTHESIZER

A **polyphonic synthesizer** has the ability to sound several notes at the same time. Synthesizers started out as monophonic instruments (see p. 78), able to sound only one note at a time. Then by the mid-1970s, the first polyphonic synths appeared, combining electric organ technology with synthesizer processing. Notable among this group of instruments was Moog's Polymoog and ARP's Omni. The Omni was a groundbreaking instrument, featuring separate strings, synthesizer, and bass synth sections, and a basic chorus effect. For the first time, musicians could play chords using synthesized string sounds—routine today, of course, but revolutionary at the time.

These synthesizer/organ hybrid instruments were then eclipsed by the arrival of genuinely polyphonic synths by the late 1970s, notably, the Yamaha CS series (CS-50, CS-60, and CS-80), and the Oberheim Two-Voice and Four-Voice. These instruments also had the ability to save individual sound programs or patches, allowing the performer to change sounds quickly during a performance. In particular, the Yamaha CS-80 is a classic from this early polyphonic period, with complete performance features including a splitable, velocity-sensitive and pressure-sensitive keyboard, polyphonic aftertouch, and a ribbon controller (see p. 109) enabling polyphonic glides and pitch-bends. This was a huge instrument weighing over 200 pounds, and is now found mostly in studios and in enthusiasts' collections. A virtual who's who of music icons have used the CS-80 in concert and/or on recordings, including Stevie Wonder, David Bowie, Peter Gabriel, Toto, and Paul McCartney. Almost all of the synthesized sounds in Vangelis's soundtrack for the movie *Blade Runner* were produced on the CS-80.

Polyphonic synthesizers took another big leap forward with the introduction of Sequential Circuits' Prophet-5 synth (see p. 99) in 1978. The Prophet-5 was an analog synth with digital programmable sound presets, and was also physically compact and lightweight. Then in 1983 Kurweil introduced their K250, which was the first widely-used digital polyphonic synthesizer. The Prophet-5 and Kurzweil K250 have been significant influences on the design of most other synthesizers and workstation keyboards, up until the present day.

PROGRESSIVE ROCK

Progressive rock, also known as **prog rock**, or simply **prog**, is a style of rock music that emerged in the late 1960s and early 1970s. This style went beyond the standard song structures of the time, creating complex arrangements and incorporating significant classical and jazz influences. Progressive rock songs sometimes have lengthy instrumental sections and abstract or conceptual lyrics. Rhythmically, the style often uses complex time signatures ("odd-time") as well as tempo changes in the middle of songs. Most progressive rock makes extensive use of synthesizers, alongside traditional instruments such as guitar, bass, and drums. Although many people associate this genre with classic 1970s bands—such as Yes, Genesis, and ELP—progressive rock is alive and well in the 21st century, with groups like Spock's Beard and the progressive metal band Dream Theater.

Our first progressive rock example is in a style reminiscent of the band Yes, and features an analog synth comping part courtesy of the ES2 softsynth (within Logic):

TRACK 56

Progressive Rock

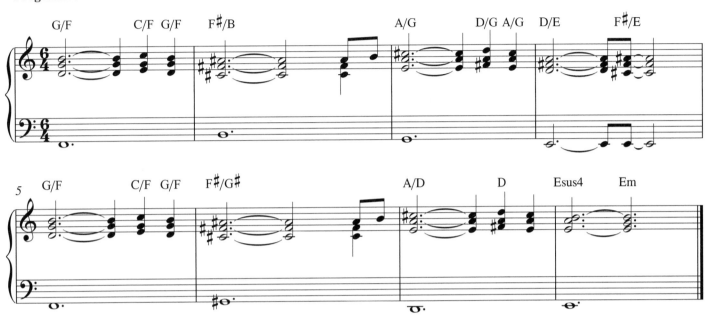

Listen to the track and you'll hear that the synth comping is on the right channel, with the other instruments on the left channel. Note that this example uses a 6/4 time signature, and has a polyrhythmic feel, combining two different rhythmic subdivisions. You can tap your foot on the quarter notes (six per measure), and the above synth part is landing on some of these beats; you can also tap you foot on each dotted quarter note (four per measure), which has more of a shuffle or "12/8" feel. Go ahead and try it! You'll also notice that there is no written key signature. The keys are changing frequently in this example, so a key signature would have been arbitrary and not particularly helpful. These types of key changes are common in more advanced progressive rock styles.

On the left channel, the backing band includes an organ arpeggio part from Native Instruments' B4, a Moog-style synth bass from Applied Acoustic Systems' Ultra Analog, and acoustic drums from Fxpansion's BFD2 virtual drum instrument.

Harmony/Theory Notes

This is a two-handed synth comping part, with the left hand playing the roots of the chords, and the right hand using upper structure triads and alternating triads. For example, in measure 1 in the treble clef we are alternating between G and C major triads, which are built from the 9th and 5th respectively of the implied F major chord, whose root is in the bass clef. Similar alternating triad movements are used in measures 3, 5, and 7, again all implying major harmony. In measure 4, the D major triad built from the 7th (with respect to the root E) implies a suspended dominant chord, which moves to the F♯ major triad built from the 9th (implying a major chord with upper extensions—9th, ♯11th, and 13th). In measures 2 and 6, the F♯ major triad is built from the 5th of a B major chord, and the 7th of a G♯ suspended dominant chord, respectively.

Further Reading

For more information on the use of alternating triads in rock styles, please check out my keyboard method *The Pop Piano Book*, published by Hal Leonard Corporation.

Our next progressive rock example is in a style reminiscent of the band Genesis, and features a soft analog lead synth sound from Applied Acoustic Systems' Ultra Analog softsynth:

TRACK 57

Progressive Rock

Listen to the track and you'll hear that the arpeggiated synth lead is on the right channel, with the rest of the band on the left channel. This type of synth part, together with the syncopated rhythm section and the 12-string acoustic guitar comping, is all typical of 1970s prog-rock. Again, no key signature is shown, as there are a number of key changes throughout the example.

On the left channel, the backing band includes Scarbee's Red Bass, MusicLab's RealGuitar (playing the acoustic 12-string), Fxpansion's BFD2 virtual drums, and Native Instruments' B4 virtual organ.

Harmony/Theory Notes

This solo part is based on chordal arpeggios and scale tones, with some resolutions within the chords. For example, in measure 1 the 3rd of the Dm chord (F) moves to the 9th or 2nd (E) of the Dsus2 chord; in measure 2 the 4th of the Asus4 chord (D) moves to the 3rd of the A chord (C#), and so on. This resolution technique adds interest and sophistication to the synth line, and is commonly used in progressive rock and other styles.

PROPHET-5

The **Sequential Circuits Prophet-5** is a famous analog synthesizer, in production from 1978 until 1984. This unit was polyphonic (up to five notes at once) and was one of the first synthesizers featuring patch memory, for instant storage and recall of sounds. This, together with its extensive modulation capabilities and great sound, made the Prophet-5 an instant classic. This synth has been used on countless recordings, by artists such as the Doobie Brothers, Phil Collins, Level 42, Eurhythmics, and INXS.

As well as having a characteristically warm analog quality, the Prophet-5 was particularly noted for its bass sounds and sound effects. There were three revisions (or versions) of the Prophet-5:

- Revisions 1 and 2 have stability problems, but use SSM (Solid State Music) chips that many players claim gives these units a "fatter" sound.

- Revision 3 units are more stable, but use Curtis chips that many players feel do not sound as good as the SSM chips. Revision 3 units are capable of taking a MIDI retrofit (unlike revisions 1 and 2), and are also capable of microtonal tuning.

The legendary sound of the Prophet-5 lives on in the 21st century, recreated by softsynths such as Arturia's Prophet V and Native Instruments' Pro-53. Next up we have a music example in a funk style, featuring a synth comping part created in the Pro-53 softsynth:

TRACK 58

Funk

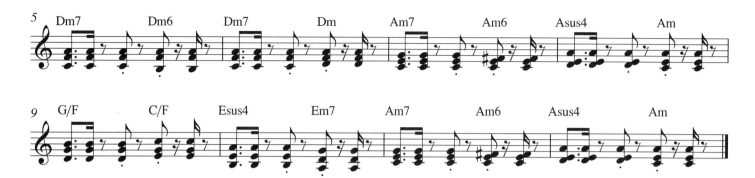

Listen to the track and you'll hear that the synth comping is on the right channel, and the rest of the band is on the left channel. This synth sound is a classic Prophet-style patch, with both ocscillators producing pulse waves (see p. 102) set to different widths, and slightly detuned for a "fatter" sound. The funky rhythm section on the left channel is courtesy of Scarbee's Red Bass (using the slap bass samples) and Fxpansion's BFD2 virtual drum instrument.

Harmony/Theory Notes

The musical form of this example is a 12-bar minor blues, in the key of A minor. The synth part uses some upper structure triads—for example, at the beginning of measure 1 the C major triad is built from the 3rd of the Am7 chord (the bass part is playing the low A, on the left channel). Similarly, on the Dm7 chord in measure 2, the F major triad is built from the 3rd of the chord. In measure 9 we are alternating between G and C major triads, which are built from the 9th and 5th respectively of the implied F major chord (whose root is again in the bass part). We are also using some interior resolutions within the chords—for example, in measure 1 the 7th of the Am7 chord (G) moves to the 6th of the Am6 chord (F♯). Similarly, in measure 2 the 7th of the Dm7 chord (C) moves to the 6th of the Dm6 chord (B), and so on. Most of the time, the synth part does not include the roots of the chords (the roots are being played in the bass part). This is a common contemporary voicing technique when the chord symbols are bigger than simple triads (i.e., four-note chords and larger).

Further Reading

For more information on the 12-bar blues form and blues keyboard stylings, please check out my book/CD combo *Blues Piano: The Complete Guide with CD!*, published by Hal Leonard Corporation.

PROTOOLS

ProTools is a music production and recording program, manufactured by Digidesign. It is one of the leading DAW (digital audio workstation, see p. 26) softwares currently available, and has become the industry standard for audio recording in most studios worldwide. Although ProTools works with both MIDI and audio tracks, its particular strength is in the audio domain (recording, mixing, and mastering).

Musicians who need to do significant MIDI work and editing on a project often prefer to do this in another DAW that has sophisticated MIDI editing capabilities (e.g., Cubase or Digital Performer), create and export the necessary audio files, and then import these files into ProTools for audio processing. So even though the manufacturers of other DAWs promote their products' ability to record, edit, and manipulate audio tracks (i.e., competing with ProTools), they nonetheless ensure that their DAWs can export a project in a format that ProTools can read, a tacit acknowledgement of ProTools' pre-eminent position in the recording industry. This audio format is called OMF (Open Media Framework) and was introduced by Avid Technology, Digidesign's parent company. OMF format is supported by other leading DAWs such as Cubase, Logic, Digital Performer, and Sonar, among others.

With the release of ProTools 8 in 2009, Digidesign added significant MIDI editing and virtual instrument capability, in an aggressive attempt to complete with other DAWs (such as Logic and Cubase) in these areas. It will be interesting to see whether these features will make ProTools as a serious player in the sequencing and "music creation" market as it currently is in the recording and mixing realm.

ProTools runs on both Macintosh and Windows computers. Here's a screen shot of a typical ProTools "arrange" page:

ProTools comes in three basic configurations: HD, LE, and M-Powered. HD is the high-end professional ProTools system, and uses a mixture of hardware and software. Most of the audio processing is done on special DSP "cards" installed in the host computer, with external rack-mountable interfaces handling the audio input and output. LE is the "consumer-level" ProTools system, which performs all processing on the host computer's CPU (without DSP cards), with audio I/O handled by a USB or FireWire interface (this is similar to how other DAWs work). The ProTools LE software is a scaled down version of the HD software, with a smaller maximum track count, and without surround-sound capabilities. M-Powered is a version of ProTools LE that works with a range of M-Audio interfaces. (M-Audio was acquired by Avid in the mid-2000s).

Effects processing and virtual instruments are available in ProTools by using plug-ins. These may be processed by the DSP cards (as TDM format plug-ins) in a ProTools HD system, or by the host computer (as RTAS format plug-ins) in a ProTools LE or M-Powered system. See p. 94 for more information on plug-ins and their formats. Digidesign has released a series of virtual instrument plug-ins that work only in ProTools, such as Strike (virtual drum instrument), Eleven (guitar amp modeller), Velvet (virtual electric piano), and various others.

PULSE WAVE

A **pulse wave** is a basic type of waveform (see p. 102) available on many synthesizers. It has similar properties to a square wave (see p. 122), except that it does not have the perfectly symmetrical shape of a square wave:

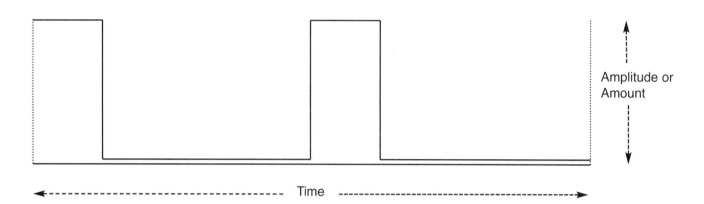

Amplitude or Amount

Time

Pulse and square waves are either "all the way on" or "all the way off," and the ratio of how much time the waveform spends on and off is known at the duty cycle. (As the square wave is a symmetrical shape, its duty cycle is always 50%.) In the above pulse wave example, the duty cycle is 25%, as the wave is in the "on" position 25% of the time. Square waveforms in general have a hollow-sounding characteristic. The pulse wave is a thinner, narrower-sounding version of the square wave and re-introduces some even harmonics, compared to the square wave, which has odd harmonics only. Due to their thinner sound, pulse waves are often used as the basis for programming clavinet sounds on analog synthesizers.

The width of a pulse wave may also be cyclically modified over time, normally by a low-frequency oscillator (LFO, see p. 71). This is known as pulse width modulation, and imparts a detuning or chorus-like effect to the sound. This technique is often used when programming strings or bass drone sounds, to add more motion and realism. Technical note: Pulse width modulation is actually equivalent to the difference between two sawtooth waves (see p. 115).

On the CD track, we start out with a square wave (from the ES2 softsynth within Logic), and then modify the duty cycle to create two different pulse waves. So the following example is played three times in total:

TRACK 59

- The first performance of this phrase uses a pulse wave with a 50% duty cycle (i.e., a square wave), which has a rounded, hollow sound.

- The second uses a pulse wave with a 25% duty cycle, which results in an edgier, narrower sound.

- The third uses a pulse wave with a 10% duty cycle, resulting in a thinner, more nasal sound quality.

QUANTIZE

Quantization is an editing function that corrects rhythmic inaccuracies in a musical part being recorded with a sequencer (see p. 116), which is either software-based (i.e., a digital audio workstation or DAW, see p. 26), or a hardware unit such as a workstation keyboard (see p. 140), or a stand-alone hardware sequencer. Quantization has traditionally been applied to MIDI data ever since software and hardware sequencers were first introduced. However, with the advent of faster computers and more powerful software capabilities, quantization of audio tracks is now offered in most major DAWs.

For an example of how quantization works, let's say that you have just recorded a synth part into your favorite sequencer, but your timing was a little off (maybe some some notes were "too late" or behind the beat). Using the quantize function, you can decide how much you want to clean up the timing. (The default is normally 100%, meaning that the notes will be moved to the exactly correct rhythmic locations.) Although you might think that the 100% quantizing is what you want to do, in practice this type of "exact quantizing" can make the part sound stiff and mechanical. Though this might be fine in electronic styles such as trance and techno, it could sound too mechanical for organic styles such as traditional rock and R&B.

So for these styles, you can specify a percentage quantize (say 50%) that will move the notes just halfway toward the exact rhythmic subdivisions (normally eighth- or 16th-notes in most contemporary styles). This will normally clear up any significant "slop" in the part, while maintaining a human, organic feel. I use percentage quantizing a lot when working in DAWs such as Logic, Digital Performer (DP), and Reason. Although synthesizer workstations and hardware sequencers typically offer quantization features, they are normally not as powerful or flexible as those offered within today's software-based DAWs.

These days most DAWs also offer groove quantization features, where the part is quantized according to a specified rhythmic feel or groove, which may be imported from a groove template. Also, most sequencers offer input quantization features, which will immediately quantize a part as it is being recorded. Although this may be handy in some situations, I think most players prefer the flexibility of quantizing after the part has been recorded.

The following music example is in a pop/rock style, and was created in Digital Performer (DP). On the CD this example is repeated on three different tracks, with different quantization settings. This time, the featured instrument on the right channel is an electric organ, courtesy of the Native Instruments' B4 virtual organ plug-in:

TRACK 60, 61, 62

Pop/Rock

The CD tracks 60–62 have different quantization settings applied, as follows:

- Track 60 has no quantization applied, and (as you can hear!) is a rather sloppy performance. Each instrument (organ, guitar, bass, and drums) has significant rhythmic/timing inaccuracies.

- Track 61 is the result of applying a 50% quantization to all of the instruments in Track 60. This has the effect of cleaning up the major rhythmic slop, but still retaining something of a "human feel."

- Track 62 is the result of applying a 100% quantization to the instruments in Track 60. This has the effect of cleaning up the rhythmic inaccuracies, but may be too rigidly quantized for this particular style. Let your ears be the judge.

On the left channel, the backing band includes Scarbee's Red Bass and MusicLab's RealStrat (through IK Multimedia's amp simulator plug-ins Ampeg SVT and Amplitube, respectively) and Fxpansion's BFD2 virtual drum instrument.

Harmony/Theory Notes

This pop/rock organ part is created using a mixture of 4th intervals within pentatonic scales, upper structure triads, and double-4th shapes (two consecutive perfect 4ths intervals). The 4th intervals are created from the E minor pentatonic scale (E G A B D). The upper G major triads are either built from the 3rd of the Em7 chords or from the root of the G major chords. The C-D-G voicing (from bottom to top) on the Csus2 chords is an inversion of a double-4th shape built from the 9th (or 2nd) of this chord. In measures 6 and 14, this is embellished with an interior resolution (F♯ to G), which is the flatted 5th (or sharped 11th) moving to the 5th, on this chord. This is a common sound in pop/rock and progressive rock styles.

Further Reading

For more information on using pentatonic scales, 4th intervals, and double-4th vocings over different chords, please check out my piano method *The Pop Piano Book*, published by Hal Leonard Corporation.

REAKTOR

Reaktor is a modular "music studio" software program manufactured by Native Instruments. It works as a plug-in within all major digital audio workstations (DAWs, see p. 26), or as a stand-alone application. Reaktor allows musicians to design and build their own instruments, samplers, and effects from the ground up, using a modular interface to combine the various building blocks into ensembles. It also allows the user to design the GUI (graphical user interface) for their instrument. Reaktor has a considerable learning curve, but for those who have the desire to master all its parameters and technicalities, the sky is the limit in terms of virtual instrument design.

Reaktor 5 ships with 32 pre-programmed instruments, including various synthesizers, sequencers, samplers, grooveboxes, and effects. Reaktor also has a substantial and enthusiastic user community, and over 2,000 user-developed instruments can be downloaded from the Reaktor User Library at no charge. There are not many widely available software programs that enable you to design your own instruments. Reaktor's closest competition is Applied Acoustic Systems' Tassman and Cycling 74's Max/MSP.

Now we'll listen to some music examples that explore Reaktor's vast potential.

TRACK 63

**Dramatic/
Sound Effect**

Listen to Track 63 to hear the sound of Spacedrone, an algorithmic effects instrument in the Reaktor 5 library. This effects generator produces a great range of atmospheric sound effects, from rain and wind noises to unique other-worldly textures. This instrument features up to 96 separate noise generators, each of which is then filtered and modified by an amplitude envelope before being placed in the stereo field.

TRACK 64

Industrial

Listen to Track 64 to hear the sound of Massive, a drum computer instrument in the Reaktor 5 library (not to be confused with Native Instruments' softsynth also called Massive, which has been used on various other CD tracks for this book). This instrument processes drum samples through envelopes, filters, and a "grain re-synthesis algorithm" to produce unique drum and percussion sounds. It also has a sophisticated step sequencer, with independent loop lengths for each track in the sequence. This CD track is a layered percussion groove in an industrial style, giving a good demonstration of Massive's sequencing and sonic capabilities.

REASON

Reason is a music production and recording program manufactured by Propellerhead Software. It is one of the leading DAW (digital audio workstation, see p. 26) softwares currently available. Reason runs on both Macintosh and Windows computer platforms. Unlike other DAWs, Reason's design is based on a "studio rack," into which users can insert virtual devices (instruments, mixers, and effects). With a single keystroke, the user can toggle between "front" and "back" views of the virtual rack. With the back view visible, it is possible to use virtual cables to connect the various rack components together in many different ways, enabling complex chains and effects to be created. This is particularly useful for electronic music artists, and Reason is widely used in the recording and production of trance, techno, and other electronic styles.

Reason's instruments and effects can be controlled from its own built-in sequencer, or from other DAWs (such as Cubase, Logic, etc.) using the ReWire communication protocol, developed by Propellerhead. At the bottom of Reason's screen interface (below the "virtual rack"), there is a miniature "arrange" panel available if Reason's sequencer is being used. This has a vertical list of tracks and a horizontal timeline, and is similar in function to the main "arrange" pages in other programs. However, the fact that it cannot be widened (beyond the width of Reason's virtual rack) can be frustrating to users accustomed to the large, detailed track views offered by other DAWs. Here are some screen shots of "front" and "back" views of a typical Reason virtual rack:

Reason was first introduced in 2000 and was up to version 4 by 2008. The latest version ships with several very interesting and useful softsynths, including:

- *Thor*, a semi-modular synth combining analog, FM, and wavetable synthesis, and with advanced filtering capabilities

- *Malstrom*, a synth combining granular and wavetable synthesis (see granular synthesis, p. 49)

- *NN-XT*, an advanced sampler with extensive sound-shaping and editing features

Also new in version 4 is the Combinator, which allows users to combine multiple instrument and effects modules into one. Complex device set-ups can be saved and transferred between different projects.

Among the available DAWs out there, Reason has some specific advantages and disadvantages. Its rack-style interface, great synth plug-ins, "tweakability," and loop-friendly interface and features make it a go-to program in the electronic music world. However, its inability to record audio tracks or to use third-party plug-ins (together with its rather basic "track view" display) are also significant limitations for many musicians.

Now we'll listen to a musical example in an abstract (or experimental) funky hip hop style, created in Reason. Our featured instrument is a rhythmic comping synth from Reason's Thor synth plug-in, which has a somewhat "grainy" (or low-fi) sound quality suitable for some hip hop styles:

TRACK 65

Abstract Hip Hop

Listen to the track and you'll hear that the synth comping is on the right channel, and the rest of the band is on the left channel. This example uses a swing-16ths rhythmic feel common in hip hop styles. The backing band on the left channel includes a synth bass from Reason's Subtractor analog softsynth, and a digital-style synth pad courtesy of Reason's Malstrom softsynth.

Harmony/Theory Notes

This synth part uses an important keyboard voicing technique known as "7–3 voicing," playing the 7th and 3rd of successive chords. For example, in the first half of measure 1 the synth plays the notes G and C (the 7th and 3rd of the Am7 chord). Similarly, in the second half of measure 1 the synth plays the notes F# and C (the 3rd and 7th of the D7 chord), and so on. These 7-3 voicings are a staple keyboard technique across a range of jazz, Latin, and R&B styles. This synth part also uses some 4th intervals from the A minor pentatonic scale, such as the D-G and E-A intervals in measures 4 and 8. (The G-C 7-3 voicing on the Am7 chords is also a 4th interval within the same pentatonic scale.)

Further Reading

For more information on 7–3 voicings and their use in jazz and R&B/funk styles, please check out my book/CD combos *Smooth Jazz Piano: The Complete Guide with CD!* and *Jazz-Blues Piano: The Complete Guide with CD!*, both published by Hal Leonard Corporation.

RELEASE

In a synthesizer, the **release** is the fourth or last stage of an envelope generator (see p. 41), which is a modifier normally applied to the filter (see p. 44) to control the timbre, or to the amplifier (see p. 9) to control the volume. The release is the time taken for the envelope to close (return to zero amplitude) once the note has been released on the keyboard. Most commonly, release is used in the context of the amplifier envelope, representing the time taken for the sound to stop (or "die away") once the note is released.

The following musical example demonstrates some different release times applied to the amplifier envelope. This track uses a sawtooth/pulse wave combination from the ES2 softsynth (within Logic). This example is played three times in total, with different release times as noted below:

TRACK 66

- The first performance of this phrase has an amplifier envelope release time of zero. This results in a very abrupt, clipped ending to each note.

- The second has an amplifier envelope release time of 200 ms (milliseconds). You can hear that, compared to the first repetition, the ending of each note is less abrupt, and takes a little while to die away.

- The third has an amplifier envelope release time of 400 ms. Now the release sounds noticeably longer, making the 16th notes in the phrase run into one another.

Changing the release time and/or the attack time (see p. 17) of an amplifier envelope, are among the two most common edits that synth players have to do on the fly when dialing up a patch and tailoring it for use in a specific musical situation. Learn how to do this on your keyboard synthesizers and softsynths, because there'll probably be a time when you'll need to do it in a hurry, either at a live performance or in the recording studio.

RESONANCE

In a synthesizer, **resonance** is a function that boosts or reinforces the frequencies near the filter cut-off point (see p. 44). This can dramatically increase the effect of the filter, and is a very classic and recognizable analog synth sound, particularly when combined with an LFO modulation of the cutoff frequency (see p. 71). Technically, the width of the "resonant peak" of frequencies (i.e., how broad the frequency range being boosted) is a parameter called the "Q." However, the term Q is also more loosely used simply as a synonym for resonance, so these terms end up being used interchangeably.

The following musical example demonstrates different resonance settings applied to an analog synth bass sound, courtesy of the ES2 softsynth (within Logic). This is played three times, with different resonance settings as noted below:

TRACK 67

- The first performance of this phrase has a resonance setting of zero, so the filter and envelope are acting normally with no additional boosting of the frequencies.

- The second has a resonance setting of 25%, and you can hear (in comparison to the first repetition) that the frequencies around the cut-off are more pronounced.

- The third has a resonance setting of 50%, resulting in a more dramatic frequency boost on each note.

If you then increase the resonance setting beyond a certain point, the filter will go into self-oscillation, resulting in unusual (and sometimes rather tortured!) sounds being created. This can be useful in electronic styles such as industrial music, and also in sound effects production. Use the resonance parameter on your synth with care: it may bite back, so to speak!

RIBBON CONTROLLER

In a synthesizer, a **ribbon controller** is used to modulate (control) some aspect of the sound. It is most often used for pitch-bending, although it can be used to change other parameters such as filter cut-off frequency, amplifier volume, and so on. Unlike the modulation wheel controller (see p. 78), the ribbon controller has no moving parts. Instead, the player presses a finger down on the ribbon and then, maintaining contact with the ribbon, moves the finger along its length; the amount of movement then determines the degree of effect that is applied. Some ribbon controllers are also pressure-sensitive and/or velocity-sensitive, enabling further control over the sound.

The ribbon controller is actually similar in function to the touchpad found on laptop computers, in that it registers the motion and position of the user's fingers. However, ribbon controllers normally register only linear (i.e., one-dimensional) motion, unlike computer touchpads, which register in two dimensions. Perhaps the most famous exponent of the ribbon controller is the keyboardist Keith Emerson, who used it extensively on his Moog modular system during the early 1970s. One reason the Yamaha CS-80 (see polyphonic synthesizers, p. 95) is enduringly popular is its ribbon controller, which enables players to accomplish polyphonic glides and pitch-bends with ease. Ribbon controllers have also been implemented in several synths of the 1990s and 2000s, including Kurzweil's PC161, Alesis' Andromeda, and Yamaha's Motif XS series.

ROLAND

Roland is a major electronic musical instrument manufacturer founded in 1972. Shortly afterward, the company introduced two important synthesizers: the SH-1000 (Japan's first commercial synthesizer, with an organ-like design and appearance) and the SH-3A (a monophonic instrument capable of additive and subtractive synthesis). The rhythmic synthesizer pulse on the classic Blondie hit "Heart of Glass" was recorded using a Roland SH-3A synthesizer.

Roland then introduced a series of "SH-" prefix synthesizers, culminating in the very successful SH-101 (introduced in 1981) that sold over 50,000 units worldwide. The SH-101 can be supported by a strap around the neck and shoulders, similar to the way a guitar is supported by a guitar strap, allowing it to function as a keytar. Famous SH-101 users include the Eurhythmics, Portishead, and Devo.

In the late 1970s and early 1980s, Roland introduced several popular and enduring drum machines (see p. 34), notably the CR-78 in 1978 (one of the first user-programmable drum machines), the TR-808 (heard on countless electronic music recordings), and its successor, the TR-909. Together with their TB-303 bass synthesizer, the TR-808 drum machine was a huge influence on the birth of hip hop and techno styles.

Also in the 1980s, Roland had major success with their Jupiter and Juno series of polyphonic synthesizers. The Jupiter-8 (see p. 58) was an eight-voice polyphonic synthesizer launched in 1981, and is considered to be one of the greatest analog synths ever made. The Juno-6 quickly followed in 1982, and this was Roland's first synth to use digitally controlled oscillators (DCOs) for greater tuning stability. The Juno series culminated in the Juno-106 in 1984, featuring patch memory and MIDI functions. Although the Juno-106 sported the new digitally controlled oscillators and envelope generation (see p. 41), it still used the older analog-style filters, which were considered to have a warmer—and better—sound quality. Roland's Juno synthesizers are enduringly popular, still used in the 21st century by artists such as Daft Punk, Moby, and the Chemical Brothers.

In 1987, Roland had another hit on their hands with the introduction of the D-50, which was the first widely available synthesizer workstation to use samples of real instruments (piano, bass, guitar, etc.) for the attack part of the sound, which was then "grafted" onto a synthesized waveform for the sustain part of the sound. The D50 was a major influence on the design of many other synthesizers, including Korg's best-selling M1 (see p. 72). Although the D-50 sounds are subjectively rather "grainy" or "lo-fi" by today's standards, it was nonetheless a hugely popular synth, featured on many classic 1980s recordings such as Michael Jackson's *Bad*, Jean-Michel Jarre's *Revolutions*, and Foreigner's *Inside Information*.

Roland then manufactured a 76-key successor unit to the D-50, called the D-70. This unit added better filters and good MIDI controller features for its time. I used a Roland D-70 on many gigs and sessions during the 1990s and found it to be a reliable workhorse keyboard. The 1990s also saw the introduction of Roland's JV-1080 and JV-2080 rack-mount synthesizer modules. These are excellent general-purpose sound modules that are still used in many studios and touring rigs.

Into the 21st century, Roland's Fantom series of workstation keyboards (see p. 140) is competing hard with similar products from Korg, Yamaha, and Kurzweil. Also, their highly regarded RD-300 and RD-700 digital stage pianos were upgraded in 2008, with new stereo multi-sampled piano sounds and other performance features. These machines feel and sound great, and are strong contenders if you're in the market for a performance keyboard.

SAMPLER

A **sampler** is an electronic musical instrument that digitally records fragments of audio and then lets you play them back from a MIDI controller such as an electronic keyboard, drum machine pads, or electronic drums. Using a sampler, you can record your own sounds (create your own samples) for later use, or you can import samples created by others (for example, a sampled grand piano or drum kit). These days there is a huge variety of sample libraries available, from manufacturers such as Ilio, EastWest, Vienna Instruments, and Sonic Reality. The main advantage of sampling is to get maximum realism—if you play back a good cello sample from your keyboard controller, the sample can sound exactly like the instrument being played.

A sampling synthesizer is one that can use a sampled sound or instrument as a waveform alongside other basic waveforms such as sine wave, sawtooth wave, etc. These sampled sounds can then be processed through the normal filters (see p. 44) and envelopes (see p. 41) available in conventional analog synthesis. Early sampling synthesizers such as the Fairlight CMI were very expensive, but by the mid-1980s less costly units such as Emu's Emulator and Ensoniq's Mirage began to appear.

In the late 1980s, workstation keyboards such as Roland's D-50 and Korg's M1 (see p. 72) began using sample playback technology. Short samples of instruments and other sounds were burned into the ROM (read-only memory) of these units. These sampled sounds were then available as waveforms, and could be filtered and processed as explained above (for the sampling synthesizer). The main difference was that these machines were unable to sample their own sounds. The player was limited to the sounds burned into the ROM at the factory, although some of these units could be expanded by memory cards with additional sounds.

Sample playback machines are also referred to as "romplers," because they play back sounds contained in their ROM. This technology has been used in all subsequent generations of workstation keyboards, up until the present day. As the cost of memory has decreased over the years, the amount of ROM allocated for samples and waveforms has significantly increased in modern-day keyboard synthesizers. Workstations such as Yamaha's Motif and Korg's M3 series incorporate sampling and sample-playback functions, as well as a sequencer (see p. 116), which enables the musician to create complete musical arrangements on the unit.

In the 21st century, a sampler can be any one of the following:

- A *workstation keyboard* such as the above-mentioned Yamaha Motif or Korg M3

- A *sampling groove workstation* (with drum machine pads, instead of a keyboard) such as Akai's MPC5000 or Roland's MV-8800

- A *software sampler* running as a plug-in (see p. 94) within a digital audio workstaion (DAW) host on a Mac or PC computer platform, such as Native Instruments' Kontakt (see p. 61) or MOTU's Mach Five

Rack-mounted hardware samplers such as Akai's S1000 and Roland's S-770 were popular in the late 1980s and early 1990s, but have now been eclipsed by today's software samplers and workstations.

Let's listen to a music example using sampled sounds. The Kontakt 3 software synthesizer and sampler (see p. 61) now includes some great orchestral samples from the Vienna Symphonic Library. On this track, the featured part is the sampled French horn ensemble sound:

(see p. 61)

TRACK 68

Orchestral

Listen to the track and you'll hear the French horn part on the right channel, with an accompanying cello ensemble part on the left channel. These are high-quality sampled sounds from Kontakt, which I have used on various television projects.

SAMPLETANK

SampleTank is a software synthesizer and sampler manufactured by IK Multimedia. It works as a plug-in within all major digital audio workstations (DAWs, see p. 26), or as a stand-alone application. SampleTank has a user-friendly interface and powerful sampling features for working with multi-sampled instruments and loops. SampleTank can also be used as the playback engine for other IK multimedia virtual instruments such as Miroslav Philharmonik, Sonik Synth, and SampleMoog, meaning that you can access all of these extra sounds directly from the SampleTank interface. (On my MacPro home studio setup, all of the SampleTank and Sonik Synth sounds are available whenever I run SampleTank.)

The sound content (samples) that come with SampleTank cover most of the typical sound categories, including guitars, synths, basses, drums, keyboards, orchestral sounds, and so on. In this respect, SampleTank is competing with other general-purpose software sampler/ workstations such as Native Instruments' Kontakt (see p. 61) and MOTU's Mach Five. Like these products, SampleTank is capable of reading sample files in formats like WAV, AIFF, Akai, and so on. However, as a long-time SampleTank user, I think the included sound samples are starting to sound a little dated compared to the competition. Perhaps this is because IK Multimedia's resources have been more focused on other products, like their very successful Amplitube guitar amp simulator plug-in, and the above-mentioned Miroslav Philharmonik orchestral virtual instrument.

Now we'll look at some music examples using the sounds included in SampleTank. First up is a pop/rock shuffle style spotlighting the synth lead part:

TRACK 69

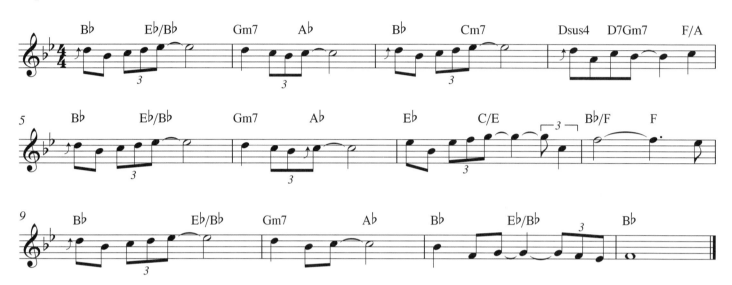

Listen to the track and you'll hear that the synth lead part is on the right channel, with the rest of the band on the left channel. This example uses a swing-eighths feel. Note that a few pitch bends (see p. 92) are used—for example, before the first note in measure 1 the pitch bend wheel is pulled back and then released, allowing the wheel to move to the "center detent" position, once the note is played. This has the effect of bending up to the desired note (in this case D).

In the backing band on the left channel, we have more SampleTank instruments: a Yamaha DX-style electric piano, a fingered electric bass sample, and an acoustic drum kit.

Harmony/Theory Notes

Once again we see a "target note" approach. For example, in measure 1 we move from the 3rd of the B♭ chord to the root of the E♭ chord (inverted over B♭ in the bass). Then in measure 2 we move from the 5th of the Gm7 chord to the 3rd of the A♭ chord, and so on. The connecting tones in between are from the B♭ pentatonic scale (B♭ C D F G).

This example is in a New Age style, featuring a warm, synthesized string pad from SampleTank:

New Age

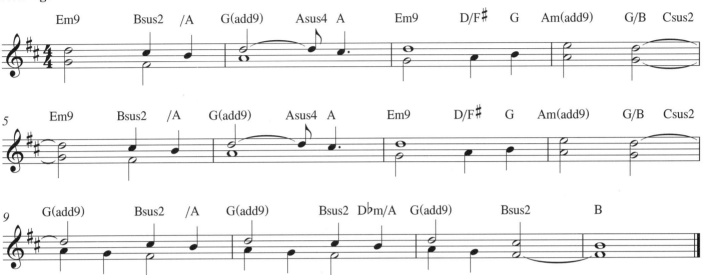

Listen to the track and you'll hear the string synth pad on the right channel, accompanying an arpeggiated acoustic guitar part on the left channel.

Harmony/Theory Notes

Note that this string synth pad uses two-note "open" voicings, as well as linear motion—i.e., one voice moving against a sustained note being held in the other voice. This helps make the part sound more realistic. The part is uses "7–3" voicings (i.e., the 7th and 3rd of the chord) on the Em9 chords, as well as root-5th voicings that are particularly effective when the 3rd of the chord is in the bass (e.g., on the G/B and D/F♯ chords).

SAWTOOTH WAVE

A **sawtooth wave** is a basic type of waveform (see p. 138), available on most synthesizers. Its name originates from its resemblance to the teeth of a saw blade:

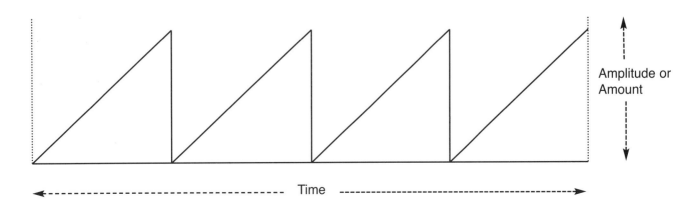

The sawtooth wave contains both even and odd harmonics (see p. 52) of the fundamental frequency. As a result, it has a harsh, buzzing sound quality. As all of these harmonics are present, this waveform is an ideal starting point for subtractive synthesis (see p. 122), for example, when synthesizing brass and string sounds.

The following CD track demonstrates the sound of a sawtooth wave:

TRACK 71

This was produced from the ES2 softsynth, within Logic. No filtering (see p. 44) or envelope shaping (see p. 41) was used, so that you can hear the raw waveform. It sounds rather harsh in this setting, but this waveform is arguably the most important building block when you're constructing synthesized sounds.

SEQUENCER

In the music world, a **sequencer** is a hardware device or software program designed to record, mix, and play back music. As today's digital audio workstations (DAWs, see p. 26) offer these features, the terms "sequencer" and "digital audio workstation" are sometimes used interchangeably. However, the term "sequencer" is also applied to various types of hardware devices that have this capability, as noted below.

At the present time, music sequencers fall into the following categories:

- *Digital audio workstation (DAW)* software programs as mentioned above, such as Cubase (see p. 23), Digital Performer (see p. 27), Logic (see p. 67), etc.

- *Workstation keyboards* (see p. 140) with sequencing capability, such as Roland's Fantom series (see p. 44), Yamaha's Motif series (see p. 80), Korg's M3 series, and Kurzweil's PC3 series.

- *Sampling groove workstations*, which combine sequencing and sampling with drum machine-style pad controllers. Leading examples are Akai's MPC5000 (a descendant of their classic MPC60 groovebox) and Roland's MV-8800.

- *Drum machines* (see p. 34), which normally contain a basic step sequencer, enabling rhythmic patterns to be composed using a grid, each step typically consisting of a 16th-note. Leading examples are Alesis' SR-18 and Zoom's MRT-3B.

- *Arranger keyboards*, which combine sequencing with automatic accompaniment features and onboard speaker systems. These keyboards are used mainly by beginners and hobbyists, although today's top arranger keyboards, such as Yamaha's Tyros2 and Korg's Pa2X Pro, have feature sets that rival many professional-level machines (and with price tags to match!).

- *Stand-alone hardware sequencers* with MIDI sequencing capability, such as Akai's ASQ-10, Korg's SQD-1, Roland's MC-500, and the Alesis MMT-8. These were popular in the late 1980s and early 1990s, but have now been largely superceded by modern-day software and hardware workstations.

 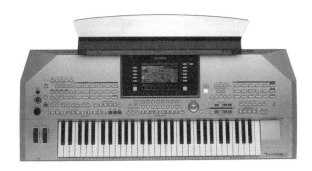

As a general rule, sequencing on the latest generation of DAW software platforms is easier and more flexible than on workstation keyboards, although the sequencers on these machines are getting better all the time, especially on the high-end Korg Oasys (see p. 84). Also, a key aspect of using sequencers within sampling groove workstations is the ability to alter the sequence and sound parameters in real time (i.e., during a live performance). Not to be outdone, software DAWs such as Ableton's Live (see p. 67) also place a heavy emphasis on manipulating sequences and loops in a live performance setting.

SEQUENTIAL CIRCUITS

Sequential Circuits, Inc. (SCI) was founded by Dave Smith in the early 1970s, and was a noted innovator in the world of synthesizers and electronic musical instruments throughout the 1970s and 1980s. Their first synthesizer was the world-renowned Prophet-5 (see p. 99), introduced in 1978. This was a groundbreaking, programmable polyphonic synthesizer with microprocessor control, and quickly became the standard for future polyphonic instruments. In 1980 SCI introduced a dual-manual, ten-voice version of the Prophet-5 (called the Prophet-10), as well as a much smaller, monophonic Prophet (the popular Pro-One, with over 10,000 units sold). The Pro-One also had a basic onboard sequencer (see p. 116), which was unusual on monophonic synths of the period.

Dave Smith was instrumental in the development of the MIDI protocol (see p. 73), and in 1982 Sequential debuted the world's first MIDI-compatible synthesizer, the Prophet 600. For the first time, you could play a note on one keyboard and hear it play back on another, with a MIDI cable connecting the two. This was first demonstrated with Prophet 600 and Roland JX-3P synthesizers at the 1983 NAMM (National Association of Music Merchants) convention. I used a Prophet 600 on many gigs in London in the mid-1980s and enjoyed its warm, analog sound, descended from its big brother, the Prophet-5.

Other important Sequential products from the 1980s include the Prophet-T8 (an eight-voice synth with a 76-note keyboard), the Six-Track (one of the first multi-timbral synths, with an onboard six-track sequencer), the Drum-Traks (a classic programmable drum machine), and the Prophet VS (which uses vector synthesis to dynamically cross-fade between multiple sound sources). The Prophet VS has an incredible range of sounds, and has been used by many top artists such as Trent Reznor, Depeche Mode, Kraftwerk, and film composer John Carpenter.

In 1987 Sequential Circuits was bought out by Yamaha, and in 1989 Dave Smith joined Korg as head of their R&D department in California. This collaboration resulted in Korg's classic Wavestation synthesizer, which combined vector synthesis with wavetable sequencing. The Wavestation has been a very popular synth from the 1990s onward, and I have used my rack-mounted Wavestation SR on numerous TV cues and studio projects.

In the 21st century, Dave Smith is again at the forefront of synthesizer technology, this time with his company Dave Smith Instruments. His current products include the Evolver (a hybrid analog/digital synthesizer, with a step sequencer) and the Prophet '08 (a re-creation of the classic Prophet-5, but with up-to-date technology and performance features).

SINE WAVE

A **sine wave** is a basic type of waveform (see p. 138), available on most synthesizers. In fact, it is the most basic type of waveform, consisting only of a single frequency, with no harmonics or overtones:

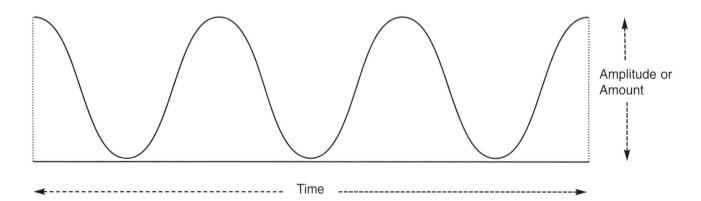

To the human ear, a single sine wave sounds pure and clean, as no other overtones are present. The sounds made by whistling, or by striking a tuning fork, sound similar to a sine wave. All other waveforms, sometimes referred to as "composite" waveforms, can be thought of as combinations of sine waves added together. This is the principle behind additive synthesis (see p. 6), which combines sinusoidal waveforms together to produce complex waveforms and overtones.

The following CD track demonstrates the sound of a sine wave:

TRACK 72

This was produced from the ES2 softsynth, within Logic. Again, no filtering or envelope shaping has been used, and you can hear the very mellow, rounded sound typical of a sine wave.

SOFTSYNTH

A **softsynth**, or **software synthesizer**, is a computer program used to generate sounds. Softsynths are also referred to as virtual instruments. These days, softsynths will function in one or more of the following capacities:

- As a stand-alone program running on a Mac or Windows computer platform (i.e., without a host program such as a digital audio workstation or DAW). For example, I can fire up the Ivory virtual piano instrument (see p. 56) as a stand-alone application on my MacPro, hook up my audio interface and MIDI controller keyboard (see p. 22), and play the instrument, with no other programs running.

- As a separately installed plug-in (see p. 94) program that can run within different DAW hosts. For example, I can launch the Kontakt softsynth and sampler (see p. 61) within multiple DAWs, such as Digital Performer (see p. 27) or Logic (see p. 67).

- As a separately installed plug-in program that can run only within Digidesign's ProTools (see p. 100) as the host. For example, within ProTools I can lauch softsynths such as Strike (virtual drum instrument), Goliath (all-purpose sampler/softsynth), and Velvet (virtual electric piano instrument). These are Digidesign products, and will not work with any other DAW host.

- As a built-in plug-in included with (and installed together with) its DAW host. For example, Reason (see p. 105) ships with various built-in softsynths, including Thor, Malstrom, and Subtractor. Another example is Logic, which ships with numerous softsynths including ES2, Sculpture, and Ultrabeat (see p. 134). Built-in softsynths like this are accessible only from within their own hosts. This means they cannot be used as a plug-in within different DAWs. (See the following comment about ReWire, however.)

- As a ReWire slave within a Rewire-compatible host. ReWire is a software communication protocol developed by Propellerhead (makers of Reason) enabling the transfer of MIDI and audio data between programs. For example, if I were working on a project in Digital Performer, but wanted to use the sounds of a Reason softsynth such as Thor, I would fire up Reason (in ReWire slave mode) so that Digital Performer could then pass MIDI data over to Reason to trigger the Thor softsynth.

There has been a huge explosion of great softsynths and virtual instrument products in recent years, using ever-larger sample libraries and with more and more sophistication and features. This is made possible by the continually faster speeds of modern-day computers, together with cheaper computer memory and hard drives. This means that if you have a reasonably well-equipped home studio (and the necessary musical skills, of course), the sky is the limit these days in terms of what you can produce.

Many musicians who want to use the great sounds of today's softsynths at their live gigs (and who don't feel like taking their laptop!) are now using the Muse Receptor, which is a "hardware plug-in player." Essentially, this is a rack-mounted computer in which your favorite plug-ins are installed. You then take it to the gig, connect it to your keyboard controller, and it functions just like a MIDI sound module (see p. 121). The stability and flexibilty of the Receptor have made it a hot favorite among touring professionals, as well as in studios where it is used to lighten the CPU load on the main computer system.

SONAR

Sonar is a music production and recording program manufactured by Cakewalk. It is one of the leading DAW (digital audio workstation, see p. 26) softwares currently available. Sonar runs only on the Windows computer platform. Here's a screen shot of a typical "arrange" page within Sonar:

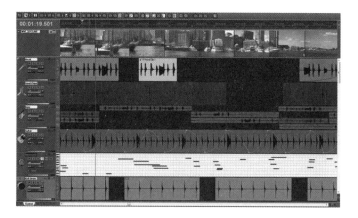

Sonar started off as a MIDI sequencer program called Cakewalk (manufactured by Twelve Tone Systems) in the late 1980s. It was originally developed for the DOS operating system, before being adapted for Windows. At first, Cakewalk was just a MIDI-based sequencer (like early versions of Cubase and Performer), but then added audio processing with successive versions of Cakewalk Pro Audio during the 1990s. In the 21st century, the company began to be referred to simply as "Cakewalk" (after their best-known product), although they did not officially change their legal name (from Twelve Tone Systems to Cakewalk) until 2008. Meanwhile, their sequencer program was also renamed, from Cakewalk to Sonar.

Sonar is currently up to version 8 for their Producer and Studio editions, and version 7 for their Home Studio editions. The version 8 Producer edition is their flagship product, with end-to-end 64-bit processing, new virtual instruments (including the very interesting Z3TA+ "waveshaping" softsynth), new mastering plug-ins, and AudioSnap quantization of multitrack audio files. Sonar is the first commercially available DAW to use 64-bit processing. This has been the centerpiece of a recent ad campaign by Cakewalk, in an attempt to gain some market share from Digidesign's ProTools (see p. 100).

The Home Studio editions emphasize ease of use and are aimed at beginners and hobbyists. However, they are quite good value for their price, with the necessary recording, editing, and quantization features, and a good entry-level selection of virtual instruments and effects.

Corporate note: In 2008 Roland (see p. 110) acquired a majority interest in Cakewalk, and the company's logo was then changed to "Cakewalk by Roland."

SOUND MODULE

A **sound module**, also referred to as a **tone generator**, is an electronic musical instrument or synthesizer without a keyboard or other playable interface. In order to play the sounds in the unit, a MIDI controller (normally a keyboard, see p. 22) needs to be connected to the unit, using a MIDI cable. Then when you play the controller keyboard, a sound is produced from the module. In my teaching studio, my students play on a Roland A80 keyboard controller that is MIDI'd to a Kurzweil Micropiano sound module, which is in turn connected to my mixer and speaker system. So when the student presses a key on the Roland A80, they actually hear the piano sound coming from the Micropiano. Although this module is now discontinued by Kurzweil, its excellent piano sounds have stood the test of time, and the Micropiano is still found in many home studios and live performance setups.

Hardware or software sequencers (see p. 116) may also connect to sound modules, in order to play back pre-recorded sequences or parts. Before the advent of computer-based virtual instruments, all MIDI sequencing was done by triggering external devices such as keyboard synthesizers, sound modules, and drum machines. Most sound modules are rack-mountable, although some fit in a half-space rack or are intended for tabletop use.

Sound modules can use different technologies to create sounds. A sound module may be a sampler (for example, the Roland S-770), or a synthesizer (for example, the Clavia Nord rack), or a "rompler" or sample-playback device (like the Kurzweil Micropiano). Drum modules are sound modules containing drum and percussion sounds, like the popular Alesis D4 and DM5 rack-mount units. Unlike drum machines, drum modules do not have pad controllers or sequencing/pattern playing capability.

In the 21st century, fewer hardware sound modules are being manufactured, as more people are using software instruments and samplers. However, rack-mount module versions of Roland and Yamaha workstation keyboards are available (Roland's Fantom-XR and Yamaha's Motif-Rack XS, respectively). In the 2000s we have also seen updated versions of classic synths, with rack-mount module versions available. For example, Dave Smith Instruments' Prophet '08 is a modern re-creation and enhancement of the classic Prophet-5 synthesizer (see p. 99), and this instrument also has a rack-mount module equivalent, the Prophet '08 Module:

Another example is Moog Music's Minmoog Voyager, a modern re-creation of the classic Minimoog (see p. 74). This instrument also has a rack-mount module equivalent, the Voyager Rack Mount Edition.

SQUARE WAVE

A **square wave** is a basic type of waveform (see p. 138), available on most synthesizers. It has a symmetrical wave shape, which alternates instantaneously between two amplitude levels:

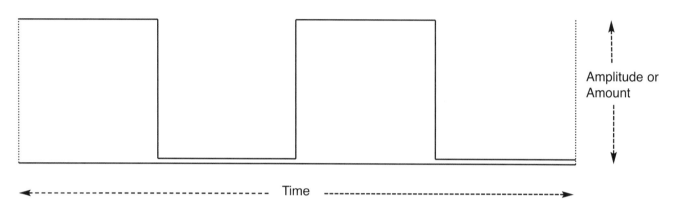

The square wave contains only odd integer harmonics of the fundamental frequency. Both square and pulse waves (see p. 102) are either "all the way on" or "all the way off," and the ratio of how much time the waveform spends on and off is known at the duty cycle. Since the square wave is a symmetrical shape, its duty cycle is always 50%. Square waveforms in general have a hollow-sounding characteristic, and are often used as a starting point for wind instrument sounds in conventional analog synthesis. Also, square waveforms can be useful when synthesizing overdriven electric guitar sounds. This is because guitar distortion effects tend to "clip" the outer parts of the waveform, which then more closely approximates a square wave as more distortion is applied.

The following CD track demonstrates the sound of a square wave:

TRACK 73

This was produced from the ES2 softsynth, within Logic. Again, no filtering or envelope shaping has been used, and you can hear the very "hollow" sound typical of a square wave.

SUBTRACTIVE SYNTHESIS

Subtractive synthesis is a method of synthesis where harmonic content is subtracted from an oscillator waveform rich in harmonics by using a filter (see p. 44). This is the method of synthesis pioneered by the early analog synthesizers during the 1960s and 1970s. This can be compared to how the human voice works: the vocal cords (equivalent to an "oscillator") generate the raw sound, and the throat and mouth (equivalent to a "filter") shape the sound by removing (or attenuating) some of the frequencies.

A common subtractive synthesis technique is to take a sawtooth waveform (see p. 115) containing the fundamental frequency and all of the harmonics, and send it through a low-pass filter that attenuates the upper frequencies beyond a designated cut-off point. Resonance (see p. 108) may then be applied, to accentuate the frequencies around the cut-off point. In this way, the timbre of an acoustic instrument may be simulated, or an entirely electronic sound may be created.

In classic analog synthesizers, subtractive synthesis was applied to basic waveforms such as sawtooth (see p. 115), square (see p. 122), pulse (see p. 102), and triangle (see p. 132) waves. However, beginning in the late 1980s with groundbreaking synthesizer workstations such as Roland's D50 and Korg's M1 (see p. 72), sampled waveforms (digitally recorded fragments of real instruments) became available as raw material for subtractive synthesis, alongside the basic traditional waveforms. Nowadays hardware and software synthesizers can use many complex waveforms and samples as the starting point for subtractive synthesis.

Now we'll hear an example in a pop/rock style, which demonstrates the filtering inherent in analog synthesis. Here the featured instrument is a brassy analog synth, from the ES2 softsynth within Logic:

TRACK 74

Pop/Rock

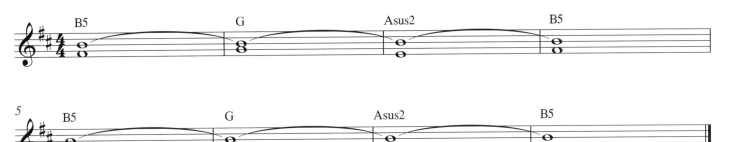

Listen to the track and you'll hear that the analog synth is on the right channel, with the rest of the band on the left channel. Note that during the first four measures, the synth has the bright, buzzy character typical of a sawtooth wave, as the filter is mostly open at this point. Beginning in measure 5 the filter then gradually closes, which subtracts (or attenuates) the frequencies above the cut-off point. This has the effect of progressively darkening the sound. The filter being used here is the conventional low-pass filter (see p. 44).

On the left channel, the backing band includes a fingered electric bass sample, courtesy of the EXS24 software sampler (again within Logic).

SUSTAIN

In a synthesizer, the **sustain** is the third stage of a conventional envelope generator (see p. 41), which is a modifer normally applied to the filter (see p. 44) to control the timbre, or to the amplifier (see p. 9) to control the volume. Unlike the attack, decay, and release envelope stages (see individual entries for these), the sustain is a level parameter, controlling the level or amplitude of the envelope for as long as the note is sustained (i.e., held down on the keyboard).

When sustain is used in the context of the filter envelope, it represents the brightness level of the sound after the attack and decay stages of the filter envelope have occurred. When sustain is used in the context of the amplifier envelope, it represents the volume level of the sound after the attack and decay stages of the amplifier envelope take place. Again it's important to bear in mind that these parameters are interconnected—for example, if the sustain level is too low in your amplifier envelope, you may not get to hear the brightness level that you expect from your filter envelope.

The following musical example demonstrates some different sustain levels applied to an amplifier envelope. This track uses an analog synth sound from the ES2 softsynth (within Logic). This example is played three times in total, each with the same attack, decay, and release times (0, 350 and 0 milliseconds respectively), and different sustain levels as noted below:

TRACK 75

- The first performance of this phrase has an amplifier envelope sustain level of zero. After the attack peak and (fairly short) decay time, the sound quickly dies away.

- The second has an amplifier envelope sustain level of 70%. After the attack and decay times, the volume adjusts to level a little lower than at the attack peak, for as long as the notes are held on the keyboard.

- The third has an amplifier envelope sustain level of 100%. After the attack and decay times, the volume stays at the maximum level for as long as the notes are held on the keyboard.

Changing the sustain level of an amplifier or filter envelope are very common edits that synth players have to do "on the fly" when dialing up a patch and tailoring it for use in a specific musical situation such as a live performance or recording. Again, it's recommended that you learn how to do this on your keyboard synthesizers and softsynths.

SYNTH-POP

Synth-pop is a contemporary music style that emerged in the late 1970s and flourished and developed during the 1980s. Synthesizers are the dominant instrument in synth-pop, and they are mainly used to create synthetic and artifical textures (i.e., rather than to emulate the sound of acoustic instruments). In particular, the new and exciting sound of digital synths such as Yamaha's DX7 (see p. 36) were prominently featured on 1980s synth-pop songs, especially the rather over-used DX7 synth bells! Songs in this style are often very melodic, and for the most part use conventional (verse-chorus-bridge-etc.) song structures. Seminal synth-pop artists include Duran Duran, the Human League, Tears for Fears, Howard Jones, and the Thompson Twins.

Our first synth-pop example is in a style reminiscent of Howard Jones, and features a digital FM-style synth comping part courtesy of the ES2 softsynth (within Logic):

TRACK 76

Synth-pop

Listen to the track and you'll hear that the digital synth comping is on the right channel, with the rest of the band on the left channel. This synth comping part has a bright, digital sheen, using basic triads and arpeggios with some rhythmic anticipations, all typical of 1980s synth-pop. On the left channel, the backing band includes a light synth brass comping part and an analog pulse wave synth bass, both from the EXS24 software sampler within Logic.

The next synth-pop example is in a style reminiscent of the Thompson Twins, this time featuring a digital FM-style lead/melody synth part from the EXS24 software sampler:

TRACK 77

Synth-pop

Listen to the track and you'll hear that the digital synth lead/melody is on the right channel, with the rest of the band on the left channel. Again, this synth sound has a bright, digital quality typical of the style. On the left channel, the backing band includes an arpeggiated synth comping part and an analog synth bass (both from the EXS24 software sampler within Logic), as well as an electric guitar courtesy of MusicLab's RealStrat virtual guitar instrument.

Harmony/Theory Notes

A "target note" approach is used in this synth part. For example, we move from the 5th of the A chord (E) in measure 1, to the 5th and 3rd of the F♯m7 chord (C♯ and A) in measure 3, to the 3rd of the G chord (B) in measure 5, and so on. The connecting tones in between are all from the A major scale.

TECHNO

Techno is an electronic dance music style that emerged in the mid-1980s and continues to evolve into the 21st century. Modern techno emphasizes synthetic and manipulated sounds, often with little or no harmonic structure, as opposed to trance (see p. 128). Like all electronic music styles, techno makes extensive use of samplers, sequencers, synthesizers, and drum machines. Most techno tracks use fast tempos. (Around 135–155 beats per minute is typical.) Techno is a mostly instrumental style, and designed to be DJ-friendly so that successive tracks can be combined in a continuous DJ set.

The main unifying element in techno is the kick drum part (normally played on each beat) and the hi-hat pattern (on every second eighth note, or upbeat). This is descended from house music (see p. 54), which is in turn descended from disco styles. Compared to these styles, however, techno is much more synthetic-sounding and less organic. Techno originated in Detroit with producers using classic drum machines such as Roland's TR-808 and TR-909, and hardware sequencers such as Korg's SQD1 and Roland's MC-50. Nowadays, techno artists and DJs perform live using loop-friendly digital audio workstations (DAWs, see p. 26) such as Ableton's Live (see p. 67) and Propellerhead's Reason (see p. 105). This 21st-century performance style is sometimes referred to as "laptronica."

Now we'll look at a couple of techno instrumental examples, and spotlight some synth parts on each. Our first example was created in Logic, and uses Logic's internal sounds and plug-ins (apart from a digital synth pad from Native Instruments' Massive softsynth). On this track we're featuring a staccato, percussive synth part:

TRACK 78

Techno

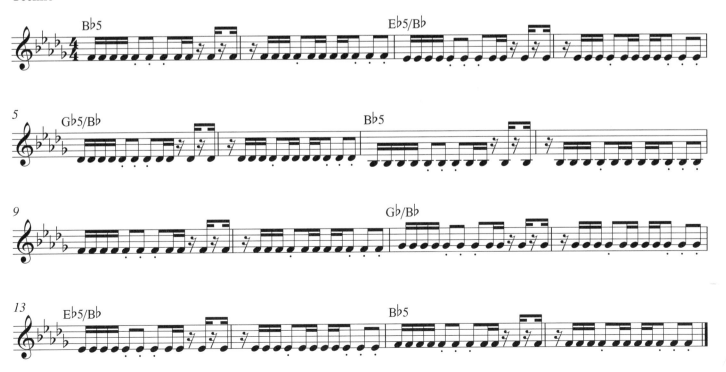

Listen to the track and you'll hear that the staccato synth part is on the right channel, with the other instruments on the left channel. The analog synth bass (on the left channel) is also playing a busy octave pattern, with the filter cyclically opening and closing over time, a commonly used sound in techno styles.

Our next techno example was created in Reason, this time featuring an electronic string synth part:

TRACK 79

Techno

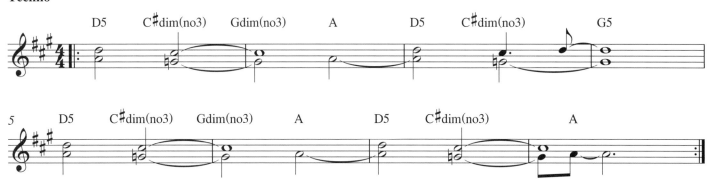

Listen to the track and you'll hear that the string synth is on the right channel, with the other instruments on the left channel. The string synth was produced using the "Phasing Strings" sound from Thor, the great new softsynth included with Reason 4. On the left channel we have some more great Reason softsynth sounds, including a very aggressive, filtered synth bass from the "graintable" Malstrom synth, and (on the second repeat) a staccato analog synth figure from Subtractor.

Harmony/Theory Notes

Note the very open, spacious quality of these two-note synth voicings, using mostly 4th and 5th intervals, with some tension due to the augmented 4th/diminished 5th intervals over the diminished chords.

TRANCE

Trance is an electronic dance music style that emerged in the late 1980s, and is still going strong in the 21st century. Trance is derived from a combination of other styles such as house (see p. 54) and techno (see p. 127), as well as ambient electronic music. Like techno, trance features synthetic sounds, but with much more emphasis on melodic phrases and harmonic progressions, and favoring minor scales and arpeggios. Like all electronic music styles, trance makes extensive use of samplers, sequencers, synthesizers, and drum machines. Most trance tracks use fast tempos, typically 130–165 beats per minute.

Although many trance tracks are instrumental, a significant percentage of trance music makes heavy use of vocals. Because this style uses more melody and harmony than certain other electronic music styles, care is needed when blending from one track to the next, as would be the case in a typical DJ set. For this reason, trance tracks are normally constructed with sparser intros and outros. Trance records also make heavy use of effects (see p. 39) on the synthesizer parts, sometimes at extreme settings to create other-worldly sounds.

Like techno and house styles, trance tracks normally place a kick drum part on each beat and a hi-hat on every second eighth note. Snare drum rolls are used to transition between phrases, which are often 32 measures in length (or longer). Although early trance artists made extensive use of vintage analog synthesizers and equipment, these days most trance producers use digital audio workstations (DAWs, see p. 26) such as Reason (see p. 105) and Live (see p. 67) to create their tracks.

Now we'll look at a couple of trance instrumental examples, and spotlight some synth parts on each. Our first example was created in Logic, and uses Logic's internal sounds and plug-ins. On this track we're featuring an arpeggiated synthesizer part:

TRACK 80

Trance

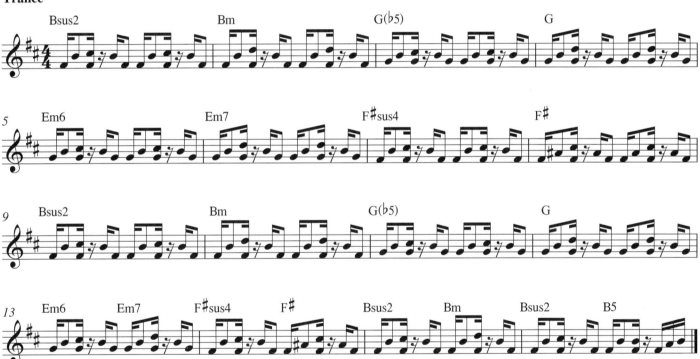

Listen to the track and you'll hear that the synth arpeggio part is on the right channel, with the other instruments on the left channel. This very bright, edgy synthesizer sound comes from the EXS24 software sampler, and is a signature trance music sound. On the left channel we have a fat Prophet-5-style analog synth bass, and an analog synth pad with an envelope applied to the filter (listen to its timbral change over time), courtesy of the ES2 softsynth.

Harmony/Theory Notes

Note this chord progression is in the key of B minor, and uses a i–♭VI–iv–V chord progression. This type of minor key progression is common in trance styles. The use of 16th-note syncopations in this figure (together with the fast tempo) creates a "busy" feel often heard in trance music. Also note the linear resolutions occuring in this part: for example, the C♯ in the Bsus2 chord (measure 1) moves to the D in the Bm chord (measure 2), the C♯ in the G(♭5) chord (measure 3) moves to the D in the G chord (measure 4), and so on.

Our next trance example was created in Reason, using its included softsynths Thor, Malstrom, and Subtractor. This time we're featuring a staccato synth comping part:

TRACK 81

Trance

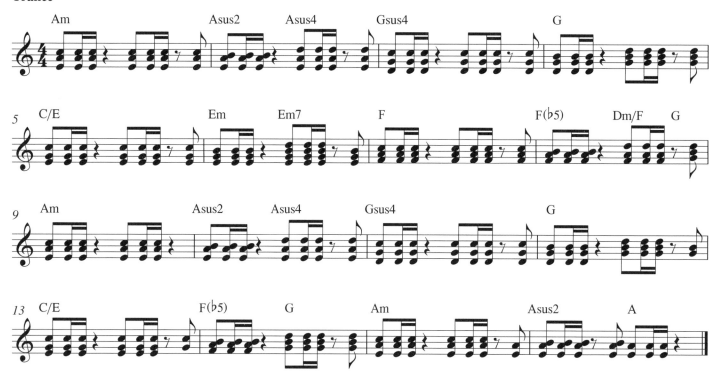

Listen to the track and you'll hear that the staccato comping synth is on the right channel, with the other instruments on the left channel. The comping synth was produced using the "Epic Poly" sound from Thor, which has already found its way onto many electronic dance tracks. On the left channel we have an FM-style synth bass from Malstrom playing on all the 16th-note subdivisions, and a Jupiter-style analog synth comping pad from Subtractor.

Harmony/Theory Notes

This synth part is a very good example of using interior resolutions within triads. In measure 1, the 3rd of the Am chord (C) moves to the 9th or 2nd of the Asus2 chord (B) in measure 2, which then moves to the 4th of the Asus4 chord (D) later in measure 2, and so on. This makes the part much more interesting and melodic than if we had just used basic triads.

TREMOLO

On a synthesizer or electronic keyboard, **tremolo** is a regular, repetitive variation in volume, normally caused by modulating the amplitude by a low-frequency oscillator (LFO, see p. 71). This term is often confused with vibrato (see p. 136), which is a regular variation in pitch. For example, the "tremolo arm" on an electric guitar actually produces variation in pitch (not volume). Conversely, the "vibrato unit" built into many guitar amplifiers actually produces variation in volume (not pitch). Go figure!

Perhaps the most obvious use of tremolo for keyboardists is when playing electric piano sounds—whether using the "real thing" or a virtual instrument re-creation of an electric piano. These days, virtual instruments such as Logic's EVP88, Applied Acoustic Systems' Lounge Lizard, and Native Instruments' Elektrik Piano re-create the classic sounds of the Rhodes (Mk. 1 and 2) and Wurlitzer electric pianos with great playability and realism. Tremolo is an often-used effect on these vintage electric piano sounds.

Now we'll check out a music example in a pop/rock shuffle style, which features an emulation of a Rhodes Suitcase electric piano, courtesy of the EVP88 virtual electric piano instrument within Logic:

TRACK 82

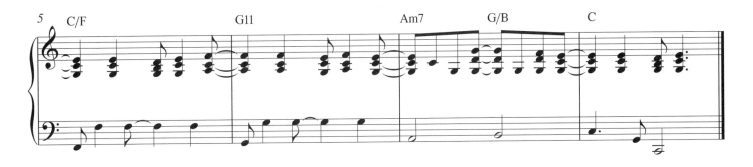

Listen to this track on the CD and you'll hear that the electric piano is on the right channel, and the rest of the band is on the left channel. This example uses a swing-eighths feel and is played twice on the track: the first time without tremolo on the electric piano, the second time with tremolo added. You can isolate the right channel to compare these two electric piano versions, as needed.

On the left channel, the backing band includes a fingered electric bass sample from Logic's EXS24 software sampler.

Harmony/Theory Notes

This electric piano part makes use of upper structure triads and "alternating triads." For example, in measure 1 in the treble clef we are alternating between C and G major triads, which are built from the 3rd and 7th respectively of the A minor 7th chord (whose root is in the bass clef). A similar alternating triad movement (between the F and C triads) is used in measure 2 on the Dm7 chord. In measure 3 we alternate between F and C major triads, which are built from the 7th and 11th of the G11 chord, and so on. These voicing techniques are typical of mainstream pop/rock styles from the 1980s onward.

TRIANGLE WAVE

A **triangle** wave is a basic type of waveform (see p. 138), available on most synthesizers. It has a symmetrical wave shape, which moves linearly between two amplitude levels:

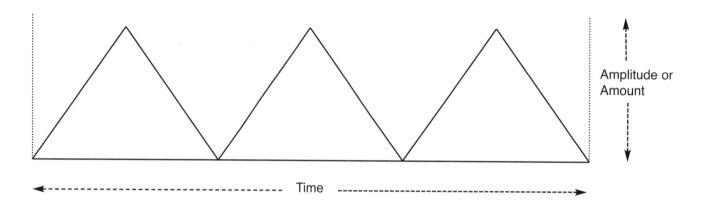

Like the square wave, the triangle wave contains only odd integer harmonics of the fundamental frequency. However, the higher harmonics "roll off" much faster than a square wave, resulting in a smoother, mellower sound that is actually closer to a sine wave. Although triangle waves sound unobtrusive by themselves, they can usefully add presence and reinforcement when layered with other sounds, such as harps and vocal samples.

The following CD track demonstrates the sound of a triangle wave:

TRACK 83

This was produced from the ES2 softsynth, within Logic. Again, no filtering or envelope shaping has been used, and you can hear the smooth sound typical of a triangle wave.

TRILL

In this book, we're referring to a **trill** as a rapid alternation between two notes. In classical or traditional circles, the term trill is used if the two notes are adjacent (i.e., a 2nd interval apart), but the term tremolo is used if the two notes are a 3rd (or larger) interval apart. Each of these situations is formally notated in its own way; we don't have the space to delve into that here. (Check out my *Blues Piano: The Complete Guide with CD!* for examples of tremolo notation.) For today's synth players, it's OK to apply the term trill a bit more loosely, to cover 2nd, 3rd, 4th intervals and so on.

The notation below shows the result of executing a trill with an exact 16th-note rhythmic subdivision. Although this is quite feasible in practice, there will also be times when the rapid performance of a trill will not line up with commonly used rhythmic subdivisions. Don't worry about that— just use your ears! Also, don't confuse the above use of the term tremolo with the use of this term to describe a regular, repetitive change in volume (see p. 131).

For the synthesizer performer, trills are typically executed while the synth is in mono mode (see monophonic synthesizer, p. 78). This means that the lower note is held down while the upper note is rapidly and repeatedly played. This is an effective synth soloing technique, particularly when combined with pitch bend (see p. 92), which affects both notes of the trill simultaneously.

The following music example demonstrates this technique, using a Moog-like analog synth lead sound from the ES2 softsynth (within Logic):

TRACK 84

This example alternates between the notes E and G, which are a minor 3rd interval apart. This is a commonly used interval in synth solos. The CD track contains two repeats of the above phrase:

- On the first pass, no pitch bending is applied, so the phrase sounds exactly as written.

- On the second pass, an upward pitch bend is gradually applied after the phrase begins, with the pitchbend wheel then returning to the "center detent" position by the end of the phrase. You'll probably recognize this sound from some of your favorite synth solos— artists such as Jan Hammer, Edgar Winter, and Rick Wakeman come to mind.

ULTRABEAT

Ultrabeat is an interesting, innovative virtual drum instrument included with Apple's Logic digital audio workstation (DAW). It is a combination of a drum synthesizer, sampler, and step sequencer. Ultrabeat is oriented toward modern electronic dance music styles, and comes with over a thousand sampled, synthesized, and hybrid drum sounds. If the onboard sounds aren't sufficient, you can also import EXS-format drum kits/samples for further editing and pattern creation.

Ultrabeat also has over 50 drum kits, each of which comes with preset patterns demonstrating different styles, which you can edit and "drag and drop" into the main Logic tracks window with ease. You can also "roll your own" drum patterns of course, using the 32-step sequencer provided. The sequencer view is very easy to use, with the drum kit elements arranged in a vertical "y axis" on the left side, and the 32 sequencer steps arranged in a horizontal "x axis" along the bottom:

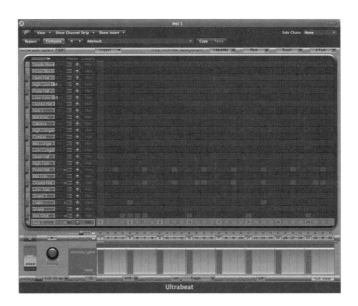

Now we'll check out a music example in an R&B/hip hop style, which uses an electronic drum kit from Ultrabeat. As well as checking out this rhythmic groove, we're also spotlighting a bluesy FM-style rhythmic synth figure from the ES2 softsynth within Logic:

TRACK 85

Listen to this track on the CD and you'll hear that the synth figure is on the right channel, and the other instruments are on the left channel. This example uses a swing-16ths feel. Listen carefully to this FM-style synth, and you'll actually hear two pitches on each note, as there's a little bit of the perfect 5th above each note mixed in. This is well-suited for funk styles using minor pentatonic and blues scales; see theory note below.

On the left channel, accompanying Ultrabeat in the rhythm section, we have an analog synth bass from Logic's ES2 softsynth.

Harmony/Theory Notes

This synth part is based on the E blues scale (E G A B♭ B D, equivalent to the E minor pentatonic scale, with the note B♭ added). This scale is then played over the chord progression, which is in the key of E minor. In measure 4 a drone note is used, with the top D repeated over the descending notes underneath. Also, various grace notes are used: the B♭ (approaching the B) in measure 4, the A (approaching the Bb) in measure 8, and so on. This is typical of blues phrasing, and imparts a bluesy feeling to this R&B/hip hop groove. Rhythmically, the part is using various 16th-note subdivisions and anticipations, which is common across a range of funk and R&B styles.

Further Reading

For much more information on blues phrasing and styles, please check out my book/CD combo *Blues Piano: The Complete Guide with CD!*, published by Hal Leonard Corporation.

VELOCITY

In the synthesizer and keyboard world, the term **velocity** is normally used in the context of **velocity sensitivity**. A velocity-sensitive keyboard is able to detect the velocity (or force) with which a key is played, and respond accordingly. For example, a grand piano has excellent velocity sensitivity, with a broad range of dynamic levels from very soft up to very loud. By contrast, a harpsichord has no velocity sensitivity, which is one of several reasons it was supplanted by the piano in the 18th century.

Most of today's electronic keyboards and synthesizers implement velocity sensitivity. Technically, this means they create a MIDI velocity message indicating how fast each note is "attacked." This is then used to control some aspect of the sound, either from the unit itself (if you are playing a keyboard synthesizer or workstation) or from another velocity-sensitive synthesizer or softsynth connected to your keyboard via a MIDI cable. Most often the velocity is used to control the volume of the sound, but other uses (changing filter cut-off point, for example) are also possible.

MIDI volume is expressed numerically as a range, from 1 to 127. When you record MIDI information using your favorite digital audio workstation (DAW), the MIDI volume is a very important component. Ideally, you want your controller keyboard to be transmitting MIDI volume uniformly across the whole range, and sometimes your controller's velocity curve may need adjusting to achieve this, depending on the physical feel of the keyboard (i.e., whether it has a light or heavy action) and your particular playing style (i.e., whether you tend to play lightly or more forcefully).

Here's an example of this concept in action: let's say you're playing Ivory (the virtual piano instrument, see p. 56) on your next gig, either from a laptop computer or from a rackmount computer device such as the Muse Receptor. A typical Ivory piano preset has up to 12 levels of samples for each note, triggered at various MIDI velocity levels (1 to 127). So if your controller keyboard is not transmitting volume data evenly across the range, you will not be accessing all of these velocity levels, which may detrimentally affect the realism and expression of your performance. This is where adjusting the keyboard's velocity curve may be helpful, to compensate for any issues regarding the keyboard feel and/or your physical playing style.

VIBRATO

On a synthesizer or electronic keyboard, **vibrato** is a regular, repetitive variation in pitch, normally caused by modulating the frequency of the note with a low-frequency oscillator (LFO, see p. 71). Vibrato is often confused with tremolo (see p. 131), which is a regular variation in volume. Synth players introduce vibrato by using different controller functions, such as aftertouch (see p. 6) or the modulation wheel (see p. 78). Some musicians subjectively describe vibrato as a "quivering" effect.

The two main variables relating to vibrato are the depth (the amount of pitch variation) and the speed (how fast the pitch is varied). Most synth players apply vibrato to single-note parts, for example when playing lead (see p. 65) or bass (see p. 18). Unless a more extreme or unusual effect is needed, you won't want to overdo the vibrato applied to lead and bass parts, because the results will not sound musical. Let your ears be the judge!

Now we'll hear an example of vibrato applied to a single, sustained synthesizer note:

TRACK 86

Listen to Track 86 to hear vibrato applied (via the modulation wheel) to an analog lead synth sound from Logic's ES2 softsynth. Note that the vibrato depth gradually increases, controlled by the amount of mod wheel movement. The vibrato speed is constant, and is determined by the pitch of the low-frequency oscillator within the ES2 softsynth.

VST (VIRTUAL STUDIO TECHNOLOGY)

VST (Virtual Studio Technology) is a software interface (or system-level format) created by Steinberg. Its purpose is to integrate softsynths and effects plug-ins within software and hardware hosts. Software hosts include VST-compatible digital audio workstations (DAWs) such as Steinberg's Cubase (see p. 23), Ableton's Live (see p. 67), and Cakewalk's Sonar (see p. 120). Hardware hosts include VST-compatible playback units such as the Muse Receptor and SM Pro Audio's V-Machine.

Nowadays VST is one of a number of competing system-level formats, among others such as Apple's AU (Audio Units), and Digidesign's RTAS (Real-Time Audio Suite) and TDM (Time-Division Multiplexing). Your choice of format will depend on which DAW host you use and which computer you have. For example, although Cubase, Live and Sonar use the VST format, Apple's Logic (see p. 67) and MOTU's Digital Performer (see p. 27) use the AU format, and Digidesign's ProTools (see p. 100) uses the RTAS and TDM formats.

When you're buying instrument or effects plug-ins for your DAW, you need to be aware of which format you need. (See p. 94 for more information on plug-ins and their formats.) If the plug-in you want is available only in VST format, and you need either AU or RTAS formats, wrapper programs are available from FXpansion (the makers of the great BFD2 virtual drum instrument), allowing VST plug-ins to be hosted in Logic or Digital Performer (AU hosts) or ProTools (RTAS host).

WAVEFORM

A **waveform** is a two-dimensional representation of a sound signal, one dimension showing amplitude (sound pressure) and the other showing elapsed time. Waveforms such as sine, sawtooth, square, pulse, and triangle waves are the basic building blocks of sound synthesis. Here is a visual summary of these basic waveforms:

- *Sine Wave* (see p. 118).
  Fundamental frequency only (no harmonics). Pure, clean sound.

- *Sawtooth Wave* (see p. 115).
  Even and odd harmonics present. Bright, buzzing sound.

- *Square Wave* (see p. 122).
  Only odd harmonics present. Hollow sound.

- *Pulse Wave* (see p. 102).
  Thinner version of square wave. Some even harmonics added.

- *Triangle Wave* (see p. 132).
  Only odd harmonics present, with higher harmonics "rolling off" faster than the square wave. Mellow sound, like sine wave.

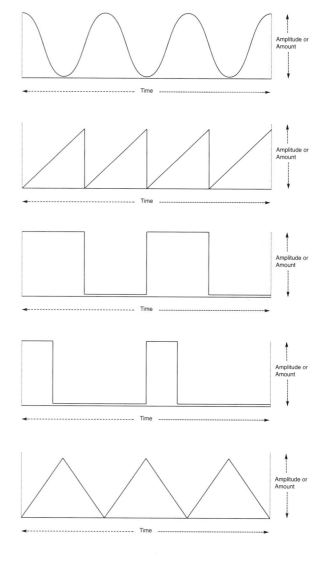

Most analog (and virtual analog) synthesizers have all of these waveforms available. For more information and audio examples, see individual entries for these waveforms.

WAVETABLE SYNTHESIS

Wavetable synthesis uses a series of short samples (of either real instruments or artificial digital waveforms) and arranges them in a sequence known as a **wavetable**. When a note is played (instead of a static waveform being heard), a wavetable sequence is then triggered, cycling through the samples in the wavetable as long as the note lasts. This allows for dynamically morphing and changing sounds over time. The effect might be subtle (such as imitating a filter sweep by using waveforms that are successively duller or brighter) or very dramatic (such as triggering a series of percussion sounds, or synth sounds with short attacks).

This technique originated in the late 1970s, with the use of digital wavetable oscillators in the PPG Wave series of synthesizers. Unique sounds were produced by these PPG synths, which were creatively used by the synth pioneer Thomas Dolby in the early 1980s. Then in 1986, Sequential Circuits (see p. 117) founder Dave Smith created the Prophet VS synth, which used vector synthesis to dynamically cross-fade between oscillators based on those in the PPG Wave.

In 1990 Dave Smith went further when designing Korg's Wavestation synthesizer, by adding wavetable sequencing to the Prophet VS design. This enabled the Wavestation to cross-fade from one wave sequence into another, creating complex, unique textures and rhythms.

In the 21st century, wavetable synthesis is alive and well in the softsynth world; the digital audio workstation Reason (see p. 105) comes with the great softsynth Malstrom, dubbed a "graintable" synth (combining granular and wavetable synthesis). Also, one of the many softsynths built in the modular music studio program Reaktor (see p. 105) is the wavetable softsynth NanoWave.

Now we'll hear an example in a pop/funk style, which demonstrates the wavetable synthesis capabilities of Reason's Malstrom. Although the synth part shown is rhythmically simple (whole and half notes), you can hear the great timbral and rhythmic (tempo-synced) effects occurring as Malstrom's "Ghost Chord" patch runs these voicings through the programmed wavetable:

TRACK 87

Pop/Funk

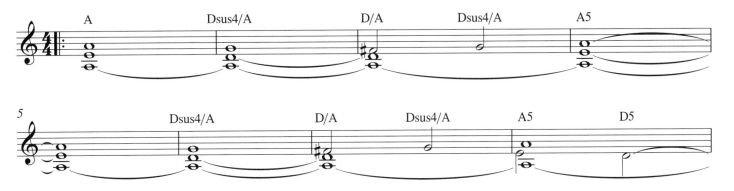

139

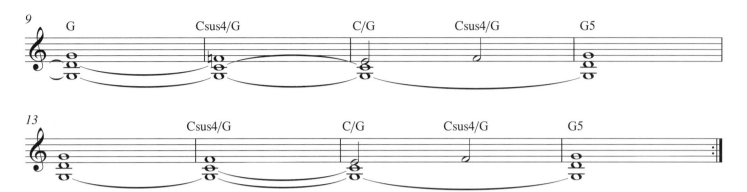

Listen to the track and you'll hear that the "wavetable" comping synth is on the right channel, with the other instruments on the left channel. Static and rhythmic comping synths enter on the left channel in measures 5 and 9 respectively, both from Reason's Thor softsynth. Then on the repeat of the whole form, an analog square wave synth bass and an FM-style bell synth join in, again both from the Thor softsynth.

Next we'll hear an example in a dramatic/sound effect style, produced on a Korg Wavestation SR module (which I still have in my studio rack after many years). Believe it or not, this sound is the result of playing only one sustained note on the keyboard, using the classic "Ancient Light" patch on the Wavestation. Great for creating an "instant film score"!

TRACK 88

**Dramatic/
Sound Effect**

Listen to Track 88 to hear some of the sound effects capabilities of wavetable synthesis, courtesy of the Korg Wavestation. This complex sound combines shifting timbres to create an other-worldly experience.

WORKSTATION

In the keyboard and computer music world, the term **workstation** refers to a piece of hardware or software that combines certain key capabilities. At a minimum, a workstation offers both sequencing (see p. 116) and sound module (see p. 121) functions, and it may also offer a sampling (see p. 112) option. A hardware workstation normally includes a keyboard and/or electronic drum pads as well.

At the present time, workstations fall into the following categories:

- *Digital audio workstation* (DAW) software programs, such as Cubase (see p. 23), Digital Performer (see p. 27), Logic (see p. 67), et al.

- *Workstation keyboards* (see p. 140) with sequencing capability, such as Roland's Fantom series (see p. 44), Yamaha's Motif series (see p. 80), Korg's M3 series, and Kurzweil's PC3 series.

- *Sampling groove workstations*, which combine sequencing and sampling with drum machine-style pad controllers. Leading examples include Akai's MPC5000 and Roland's MV-8800.

- *Arranger keyboards*, which combine sequencing with automatic accompaniment features and onboard speaker systems. Today's top arranger keyboards (such as Yamaha's Tyros2 and Korg's Pa2X Pro) have features that rival professional-level workstation keyboards.

There is also another category of equipment known as personal digital studios that you should be aware of. These are all-in-one digital multitrack recording and mixing devices. They don't have an onboard library of sounds (i.e., a sound module function as discussed above), apart from sometimes having inbuilt drum sounds and patterns available. Confusingly, these machines are referred to as digital audio workstations in some retailers' catalogs. Leading examples of personal digital studios are the Tascam 2488mk11, the Korg D3200, and the Boss BR-1600CD.

So which type of workstation should you go for? Here are some (subjective) suggestions:

- *Digital audio workstation* (DAW) software programs are still the best and most flexible way to record and produce music in a home/project studio. However, the learning curve is steeper than with all-in-one hardware units.

- *Workstation keyboards* have better and better sequencing tools these days, but are still not as powerful or flexible as a computer-based DAW, unless you have the high-end Korg Oasys.

- *Sampling groove workstations* are great for beat-intensive styles, and the high-end machines can be a fully-featured alternative to a computer-based setup. (The classic Akai MPC60 groovebox was instrumental in the creation of hip hop styles.)

- *Arranger keyboards*: See above comments on workstation keyboards.

- *Personal digital studios* are easy to use, and are great for non-electronic instruments— just plug in a microphone and hit record! These machines are good for demos and for use as an ideas scratchpad. However, they lack the flexibility and capacity of computer-based DAW setups and generally don't have onboard sounds available.

X-STATION

Novation's X-Station is one of a new generation of small, lightweight keyboard controllers (see p. 22) designed for use with a home computer recording setup. It is available in 25-key (two octaves) or 49-key (four octaves) versions, contains both MIDI and audio interfaces, and also has an eight-voice virtual analog synthesizer under the hood:

Novation's X-Station is in competition with a number of other compact two-octave keyboard controllers, including M-Audio's Axiom 25 (with eight drum/trigger pads), Yamaha's KX25, and Emu's Xboard 25.

Don't forget that, although these machines are very compact and offer good "bang for the buck," they probably will not be adequate for sequencing piano parts, due to the small keyboard size and unweighted action. However, they work great for sequencing synth-heavy electronic dance styles. The X-Station can also be used to control softsynths and plug-ins, and even your DAW software and effects!

YAMAHA

Yamaha is a leading musical instrument manufacturer, originally established in 1887. The company has since become the world's largest manufacturer of musical instruments. Their first major synthesizer was the large and very expensive GX-1, introduced in 1975. This was a high-end, analog polyphonic synth, with two five-octave keyboards and a pedalboard. Only a small number were built, and they were used by top stars such as Stevie Wonder, John Paul Jones (Led Zeppelin), Keith Emerson, and Abba.

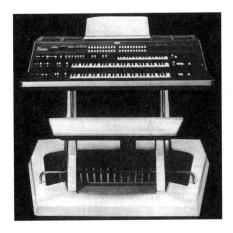

In 1977 Yamaha introduced the CS80 synthesizer (a smaller derivative of their flagship GX-1), and this unit became one of the most important synths of the 1970s. See polyphonic synthesizer (p. 95) for more information on the CS-80.

In the 1980s Yamaha began manufacturing synthesizers based on frequency modulation (FM) technology (see p. 45). The first of these were the GS1 and GS2, introduced in 1981 and revolutionary in their day; this was the first time most people had heard the bright, digital sounds of FM synthesis. The band Toto made extensive use of the GS1 on big hits such as "Africa" and "Rosanna." The GS1 and GS2 were precursors to the DX7 synth (see p. 36), which was an instant sensation upon its introduction in 1983. The DX7 in turn generated some spin-offs, including the lower-cost DX9 and DX21 synths, and the rack-mounted TX816 module, equivalent to eight DX7s in one unit.

By the late 1980s and early 1990s, synthesizers using sample playback technology (such as Roland's D-50 and Korg's M1) were very popular, and Yamaha's SY77 and SY99 synthesizer/ workstations (introduced in 1990 and 1991 respectively) took this concept one stage further by combining sample playback and FM synthesis in the same unit. This combination resulted

in some wonderful new hybrid textures, and the SY77 and SY99 were used by artists in many different styles, from industrial (Front 242, Skinny Puppy) to contemporary jazz (Chick Corea).

In 1994, Yamaha had another breakthrough with the introduction of their VL1, the first commercially available synthesizer to use physical modeling technology (see p. 89). Although this was a monophonic instrument, it broke new ground in terms of expressiveness and realism when emulating acoustic instruments.

In the 2000s, Yamaha has been busy introducing successive generations of their popular Motif workstation synthesizer (see p. 80), and its "stage piano" derivative, the S-90 series. The Motifs have also generated lower-cost spin-off synthesizer workstations—the M06 / M08 and the MM6 / MM8 (61- and 88-key versions respectively).

Z-PLANE SYNTHESIS

Z-Plane is a synthesis method developed by Emu Systems in the mid-1990s, and was an important precursor of physical modeling synthesis (see p. 89). Z-Plane synthesis is distinguished by its unique filters, which are more complex and sophisticated than traditional (analog) filters. Instead of simply attenuating the harmonic content of a waveform above (or below) a given frequency, Z-Plane filters consist of multiple sections, each allowing independent control of frequency and bandwidth. This allows the Z-plane filter to create almost any harmonic or resonant characteristic.

Z-Plane synthesis also allows for smooth movement (or morphing) between different filters over time. This can be triggered by various real-time controls, and creates dynamic and unique transformation of sounds. This technology was first implented in Emu's Morpheus rackmount synthesizer, introduced in 1993:

Z-Plane filters and morphing functions were also implemented in Emu's Ultra Proteus sound module, introduced in 1994. This noted rack-mount synthesizer included all the sounds from the previous Proteus models, and included 16 MB of sample ROM—modest by today's standards of course, but significant at the time.

CD TRACK INDEX

On each track, the featured instrument is either panned to the right (with the backing band or other instruments panned to the left), or panned to the center (if it is the only instrument on the track).

Track No.	Topic	Musical Style	Featured Instrument
1	Aftertouch	Funk	Synth lead
2	Aftertouch	Blues Shuffle	Organ (modeled synth)
3	Analog Synth	R&B/Pop	Synth bass
4	Analog Synth	Rock	Synth pad
5	Arpeggiator	Techno	Synth pad & arpeggios
6	Atmosphere	Electronic/Trance	Synth pad
7	Atmosphere	Dramatic/Film Score	Evolving synth
8	Attack	–	Synth (repeated note)
9	Bass Lines	Funky House	Synth bass
10	Bass Lines	Synth-pop	Synth bass
11	Comping	Funk	Synth comp & pad
12	Comping	Pop/Rock	Synth pad & arpeggios
13	Decay	–	Synth (repeated note)
14	Digital Performer	Electronic Dance	Synth comp
15	Digital Performer	Dramatic/Film Score	Cello ensemble (sampled)
16	Digital Synth	R&B Ballad	Electric piano (FM synth)
17	Digital Synth	Synth-pop	Horn section (sampled)
18	Drum and Bass	Drum and Bass	Synth bass
19	Drum and Bass	Drum and Bass	Synth bass
20	Drum machine	Funk	Clavinet (modeled synth)
21	DX7	Pop/Rock	Synth lead
22	DX7	New Age	Synth bells
23	Effects	–	Synth arpeggios
24	Envelope	–	Synth (brass) line
25	Envelope	–	Synth (string) line
26	Filter	–	Synth line
27	Frequency Modulation (FM)	Dramatic/Film Score	Evolving synth
28	Frequency Modulation (FM)	Trance	Synth comp
29	Glide	Classic Rock	Synth lead
30	Granular Synthesis	Ambient Electronic	Evolving synth pad
31	Granular Synthesis	Ambient Electronic	Evolving synth pad
32	Hip Hop	Jazzy Hip Hop	Synth bass
33	Hip Hop	Abstract Hip Hop	Synth bass
34	House	House	Synth comp
35	House	House	Synth piano
36	Ivory	New Age	Acoustic piano (sampled)
37	Jupiter-8	Progressive Rock	Synth arpeggios
38	Jupiter-8	Pop/Rock Shuffle	Synth pad
39	Kontakt	Rock	Synth comp & arpeggios
40	Kontakt	Dramatic/Film Score	Cello ensemble (sampled)
41	Lead	Synth-pop	Synth lead
42	Lead	Pop/Rock	Synth lead & arpeggios

43	Logic Studio	R&B/Funk	Synth comp & arpeggios
44	Logic Studio	Pop/Rock	Synth comp
45	M1	Half-time Rock	Piano (sampled)
46	Minimoog	Progressive Rock	Synth arpeggios
47	Minimoog	Funk Shuffle	Synth bass
48	Mod Wheel	–	Synth (held note)
49	Monophonic Synth	–	Synth line
50	Noise Generator	–	Synth noise
51	Pad	Neo-Soul	Synth pad
52	Physical Modeling	New Age	Acoustic guitar (modeled synth)
53	Physical Modeling	Pop/Funk	Marimba (modeled synth)
54	Pitch Bend	Funk Shuffle	Synth bass
55	Pitch Bend	R&B Ballad	Synth lead
56	Progressive Rock	Progressive Rock	Synth pad
57	Progressive Rock	Progressive Rock	Synth arpeggios
58	Prophet-5	Funk	Synth comp
59	Pulse Wave	–	Synth line
60	Quantize	Pop/Rock (0% quant)	Organ (modeled synth)
61	Quantize	Pop/Rock (50% quant)	Organ (modeled synth)
62	Quantize	Pop/Rock (100% quant)	Organ (modeled synth)
63	Reaktor	Dramatic/Sound Effect	Synth noise
64	Reaktor	Industrial	Drum/percussion samples
65	Reason	Abstract Hip Hop	Synth comp
66	Release	–	Synth line
67	Resonance	–	Synth bass
68	Sample	Orchestral	French horn ensemble (sampled)
69	SampleTank	Pop/Rock Shuffle	Synth lead
70	SampleTank	New Age	String ensemble (sampled)
71	Sawtooth Wave	–	Synth arpeggios
72	Sine Wave	–	Synth arpeggios
73	Square Wave	–	Synth arpeggios
74	Subtractive Synthesis	Pop/Rock	Synth comp
75	Sustain	–	Synth comp
76	Synth-pop	Synth-pop	Synth comp
77	Synth-pop	Synth-pop	Synth lead
78	Techno	Techno	Staccato rhythmic synth
79	Techno	Techno	Synth pad
80	Trance	Trance	Synth arpeggios
81	Trance	Trance	Synth comp
82	Tremolo	Pop/Rock Shuffle	Electric piano (modeled synth)
83	Triangle Wave	–	Synth arpeggios
84	Trill	–	Synth lead
85	Ultrabeat	R&B/Hip Hop	Synth comp/fills
86	Vibrato	–	Synth (held note)
87	Wavetable Synth	Pop/Funk	Wavetable synth pad
88	Wavetable Synth	Dramatic/Sound Effect	Wavetable synth

Take Your Playing from Ordinary to Extraordinary with the STUFF! Series from Hal Leonard

STUFF! GOOD BASS PLAYERS SHOULD KNOW

by Glenn Letsch

Provides valuable tips on performing, recording, the music business, instruments and equipment (including electronics), grooves, fills, soloing techniques, care & maintenance, and more. Covers rock, jazz, blues, R&B and funk through demos of authentic grooves. Topics include: arpeggios, chucking, fretless bass, ghost notes, isometrics, raking, slapping & popping, walking bass lines, zydeco bass and more!

00696014 Book/CD Pack $19.95
978-1-4234-3138-1

STUFF! GOOD DRUMMERS SHOULD KNOW

by Ed Roscetti

You'll receive valuable tips on performing, recording, the music business, instruments and equipment (including electronics), beats, fills, soloing techniques, care and maintenance, and more. Styles such as rock, jazz, hip-hop, and Latin are represented through demonstrations of authentic grooves and instruments appropriate for each genre.

06620108 Book/CD Pack $19.95
978-1-4234-2848-0

STUFF! GOOD GUITAR PLAYERS SHOULD KNOW

by Wolf Marshall

You'll receive valuable tips on performing, recording, the music business, instruments and equipment (including electronics), grooves, fills, soloing techniques, care and maintenance, and more. Styles such as rock, jazz, blues, R&B, and funk are represented through demonstrations of authentic grooves appropriate for each genre.

00696004 Book/CD Pack $19.95
978-1-4234-3008-7

STUFF! GOOD PIANO PLAYERS SHOULD KNOW

by Mark Harrison

You'll receive valuable tips on performing, recording, the music business, instruments and equipment, soloing techniques, music theory, and more. Styles such as rock, pop, jazz, blues, classical, and many more are represented through demonstrations of authentic piano and keyboard parts appropriate for each genre. The accompanying CD includes many of the examples in the book, performed on a variety of piano/electric piano instruments.

00311419 Book/CD Pack $19.95
978-1-4234-2781-0

STUFF! GOOD SINGERS SHOULD KNOW

by Teri Danz

From basic technique to more advanced styling, this book/CD pack is an A to Z primer for singers. As you work through the book, you'll find that it is a combination of vocal technique (exercises, breathing, pitch, harmony, and more); musical basics specifically geared towards singers (for example: ear training, chords, scales); and various styling tips (ballads, various genres).

00311490 Book/CD Pack $19.95
978-1-4234-3436-8

STUFF! GOOD SYNTH PLAYERS SHOULD KNOW

by Mark Harrison

Whether your interest lies in keyboard synths or virtual software synths, you'll receive valuable tips on techniques to help your programming and performance become more professional. The accompanying CD contains 88 tracks that represent such styles as pop/rock, blues, funk, R&B, hip hop, house, trance, dramatic/film score, and New Age. Its split-channel recording allows you to hear a full performance or to play along with only the backing band.

00311773 Book/CD Pack $19.99
978-1-4234-5768-8

FOR MORE INFORMATION, SEE YOUR LOCAL MUSIC DEALER, OR WRITE TO:

HAL•LEONARD® CORPORATION
7777 W. BLUEMOUND RD. P.O. BOX 13819 MILWAUKEE, WI 53213

Prices, contents, and availability subject to change without notice.

INTERESTED IN THE IVORIES?
CHECK OUT THESE PIANO REFERENCE BOOKS FROM HAL LEONARD

KEYBOARD PRESENTS THE BEST OF THE '80S
The Artists, Instruments, and Techniques of an Era
edited by Ernie Rideout, Stephen Fortner,
and Michael Gallant
Backbeat Books
Learn how technological developments in keyboards helped artists like Human League create entirely new sounds, and how you can recreate them today using the soft synths and recording software you already have on your computer.
00331932 . . . . $19.95
978-0-87930-930-5

88 KEYS – THE MAKING OF A STEINWAY PIANO
by Miles Chapin
Illustrations by Rodica Prato
Amadeus Press
From the selection and aging of wood to the delicate voicing of the finished instrument, this special reissue of *88 Keys* relates the story behind the instrument's intricate formation, as told by Miles Chapin, a fifth-generation descendant of Steinway's founder, Henry Engelhard Steinway.
00331739 . . . . $25.00
978-1-57467-152-0

88: THE GIANTS OF JAZZ PIANO
by Robert L. Doerschuk
foreword by Keith Jarrett
Backbeat Books
This insightful hardcover volume delves deep into the music of 88 visionaries who have made an indelible mark on the world of jazz through their mastery of the piano's 88 keys, such as Jelly Roll Morton, Earl Hines, Art Tatum, Thelonious Monk, Bud Powell, Keith Jarrett and Cecil Taylor.
00330855 . . . . $29.95
978-0-87930-656-4

THE FIFTY GREATEST JAZZ PIANO PLAYERS OF ALL TIME
Ranking, Analysis & Photos
by Gene Rizzo
Hal Leonard
This bold book steps forward and proclaims the 50 greatest jazz pianists of all time. Compiled from an extensive survey of the best jazz minds in the industry, Rizzo summarizes and presents a concise bio on the essence of these jazz giants.
00331160 . . . . $19.95
978-0-634-07416-5

CLASSIC HAMMOND ORGAN
by Steve Lodder
Backbeat Books
Professional session player Steve Lodder explores the history of this enduringly popular instrument and examines some of the best performers to get their hands on the twin manuals.
00331930 Book/CD Pack $24.95
978-0-87930-929-9

THE HAMMOND ORGAN – BEAUTY IN THE B
by Mark Vail
Backbeat Books
Traces the technological and artistic evolution of the B-3 and other tonewheel organs, as well as the whirling Leslie speakers that catapulted the Hammond sound into history.
00330952 . . . . $29.95
978-0-87930-705-9

PIANO GIRL
A Memoir
by Robin Meloy Goldsby
Backbeat Books
This is the story of one woman's accidental career as a cocktail lounge piano player. Connecting the people she has met with the places she has played and the pianos she has known, Robin Meloy Goldsby discovers the human side, for better or worse, of her audiences.
00331409 . . . . $14.00
978-0-87930-882-7

THE PIANO HANDBOOK
A Complete Guide for Mastering Piano
by Carl Humphries
Backbeat Books
With clear and easy-to-understand exercises, this guide is perfect for anyone interested in learning the piano or improving their skills.
00330987 Book/CD Pack $29.95
978-0-87930-727-1

THE PIANO IMPROVISATION HANDBOOK
by Carl Humphries
Backbeat Books
A comprehensive overview of the practical skills and theoretical issues involved in mastering all forms of piano improvisation, including classical, jazz, rock, and blues.
00332750 . . . . $29.99
978-0-87930-977-0

THE PIANO
A Complete Illustrated Guide to the World's Most Popular Musical Instrument
by Jeremy Siepmann
Hal Leonard
This is the first popular book to cover every aspect of the instrument's dynamic history, including: origins, technical developments, novelties and experiments; piano music throughout the centuries; and much more.
00330439 . . . . $19.95
978-0-7935-9976-9

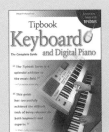

TIPBOOK KEYBOARD & DIGITAL PIANO
Hal Leonard
This book helps keyboardists understand and appreciate their instruments without getting too technical. It includes chapters on auditioning keyboards and pianos, appreciating sound, connections, MIDI, maintenance, and much more.
0033237 . . . . $14.99
978-1-4234-4277-6

VINTAGE SYNTHESIZERS – 2ND EDITION
by Mark Vail
Miller Freeman Books
The ultimate exploration of the upstart instruments that paved the way over the last four decades for today's fast-paced electronic music world. Explores the development of the modern synthesizer from 1962 on, with in-depth interviews with pioneering designers Bob Moog and Alan R. Pearlman.
00330536 . . . . $29.95
978-0-87930-603-8

FOR MORE INFORMATION, SEE YOUR LOCAL MUSIC DEALER, OR WRITE TO:

HAL•LEONARD® CORPORATION
7777 W. BLUEMOUND RD. P.O. BOX 13819 MILWAUKEE, WI 53213

www.halleonard.com
Prices, contents, and availability subject to change without notice.

0809